In her enlightening new book, *Myth Shift*, Merit Gest makes a compelling case for selecting, nurturing, and growing vital people over valuable ones in business. She throws conventional wisdom to the curb by providing leaders with new tools to lead their teams and empowering teams to deliver on their potential

> ~ **David Avrin, author of** *Visibility Marketing*

Merit Gest understands the slight shifts that MVPs make in their thinking and actions that are distinct from everyone else. This book is a great guide for MVPs who wish to shift their thinking about the myths that hold people back.

> ~ **Daniel Burrus,** *New York Times*
> **bestselling author of** *Flash Foresight*

Clever ideas and concepts that shift the notion of what it takes to reach one's full potential and accelerate success.

> ~ **Sara Canaday, author of** *You According To Them*

Looking for an innovative and culture-shifting read that will have a major impact on your business? *Myth Shift* is powerful book that does the heavy lifting for you.

> ~ **Meridith Elliott Powell, award-winning**
> **author of** *Own It: Redefining Responsibility*

Merit Gest has written exactly what business leaders would like the freedom to say to their team. At the same time, she expresses what the team wants from leadership.

> ~ **Debra Fine communication expert and bestselling author**
> **of** *The Fine Art of Small Talk: How to Start a*
> *Conversation, Keep it Going, Build Rapport -*
> *and Leave a Positive Impression*

This book peels the onion on what makes someone successful in their career. Anyone who wants to be the best in their field should read this book.

~ **Christine Hassler, bestselling author**
of *Expectation Hangover*

This game-changing book will shift your perspective about taking business situations at face value. Pay particular attention to the section on re-deciding, a must-read for leaders.

~ **Elizabeth McCormick, former U.S. Army Black Hawk Pilot,**
author of *The Pilot Method*

Every once in a while a special book comes along that may impact a company culture, sales, teamwork, and employee engagement... Merit Gest has written that book.

~ **Connie Podesta, award-winning author of**
Ten ways to Stand Out From the Crowd,
CEO of Connie Podesta Presents

Merit gives big dreamers a primer to stay on track and a foundation to keep their dreams alive.

~ **Sam Reese, CEO Vistage International**

Merit Gest does a brilliant job identifying attributes of MVPs in business that directly impact hiring and onboarding.

~ **Lee Salz, CEO, Sale Architects & The Revenue Accelerator,**
author of *Hire Right, Higher Profits*

MYTH SHIFT

Challenging The Truths That Sabotage Success

MERIT GEST

EvaGene Press

Myth Shift: Challenging The Truths That Sabotage Success
by Merit Gest

Published by EvaGene Press, Aurora, Colorado USA

ISBN 978-0-9976468-0-1

Cover design: Amjad Shahzad
Interior layout: Nick Zelinger
Author photo: Eric Weber
Illustrations: Shane Ann Connell

First Edition

Printed in the United States of America

6/2018

Everything is Not Possible. Choose Wisely.

Brad -

Thank you for being such an enthusiastic supporter of my program at MDRT. I'm honored to be part of this event and humbled that the message I shared resonated with participants /members.

I hope we get to work together at another MDRT event soon!

In the mean time ... give a shift!

Merit

To David and Jake, my MVPs.

Table Of Contents

Introduction

Building Business MVPs

My parents had a philosophy that a child grows into the meaning of their name, so they named me Merit, which means worthy of praise. Not Sunshine or Apple or Jill...Merit. I was an only child, but imagine if I had had a brother... My parents probably would have named him CEO or Billionaire!

Merit could have been a tough name for a kid. I was constantly teased. Merit, ferret. Merit, parrot. Merit gas station. Merit cigarettes. Merit Parkway. Merit Grub Control. But knowing that Merit meant worthy of praise, I lived up to it just fine, thank you very much.

This has been my lifelong quest, becoming a person worthy of praise and growing into the name Merit. Over the past twenty years, I have observed CEOs, entrepreneurs, managers, and salespeople in a variety of industries, including manufacturing, banking, professional services, and technology, among others. I have many times solicited answers to these three questions:

- What is it that makes somebody worthy of praise?
- What is the worst business advice you've ever heard?
- When you've found yourself on the wrong path, how did you turn it around?

I looked at the top achievers, the people whom you would know and expect to be on the list, and I also researched some unsung heroes. This book is the result of what I have discovered during the past two decades.

When people are grounded in the four specific areas that this book addresses, four fundamental myths that could use a shift in thinking, you have a better experience of them, and they have a better experience of everything that they're doing. They accomplish more, they get there faster, they bounce back from adversity sooner, and they have more fun.

The person on a sports team who earns the most praise and acknowledgment is known as the Most Valuable Player (MVP). Sadly, we don't have such cool titles in the business world. Employee of the Month just doesn't have the same appeal. Let's borrow the MVP title from the world of sports but put our own business spin on it.

Though business may be considered a *game*, it's not likely that you are referred to as a *player*. You are a person (at least until this book is available for sale on other planets). If you are receiving a paycheck from a company or a commission check from a client, you are providing value, so that's not really a game-changer in the area of business. Being valuable to your organization today isn't the job security that it once was.

What customers, clients, and companies want from their people, partners, and providers is someone who is not just valuable, they want someone who is vital. Vital is defined as *necessary, indispensable, essential.* Your heart is not a valuable organ, it's a vital organ. You want to be known as someone who is vital, the heart of your organization.

Be the Most Vital Person for your customers and clients. Be the Most Vital Person among your team. The distinction between being valuable and vital is night and day. Valuable companies lose business to competitors, but those that are vital to their customers keep them. Valuable people have lost jobs, deals, and dollars. Vital people will never be short on cash or clients. Strive to be your organization's Most Vital Person by shifting your thinking about some of the most common business myths.

Throughout the rest of this book when I use the term MVP, consider it to mean Most Vital Person.

After years of studying what makes someone an MVP in the business world, I have condensed that learning and those real-world concepts into the information found in this book to help you on your journey to becoming worthy of praise.

I know that you may already be the MVP of your business, so use this book to help you distinguish what you do that is different from what others do. This book will also give you the tools that you need to help others on your team, because when everyone around you is qualified to be the MVP, business gets to be real fun real fast.

In this book I'm going to share with you four specific myths that MVPs have shifted to their advantage. Changing their thought process is what top performers and MVPs, past and present, across myriad industries, do and it is what will make you more productive, promotable, prosperous, powerful, and thus more worthy of praise in business.

Before you get started, if I asked you to guess what the four myths are, you might say some version of what numerous successful business people have told me. It is a myth that you need to: be more decisive, be more proactive, be more positive, and be more present.

Being more decisive, being more proactive, being more positive, and being more present are good tips, great business advice, heck...terrific suggestions for life in general. But wait, there is a fundamental flaw here...

What I learned from my research is that if you accept these myths as the gospel, they may hurt you. What? How could being more decisive, more proactive, more positive, or more present hurt you? How could these ideas be a bad thing?

In order to win more business, flourish during change, move up faster, and go further in your career, it is important that you do not always take things at face value. Instead, consider the advice through the filter of your own experience.

The purpose of this book is to give you a chance to re-examine this business advice with just enough of a twist to take it from trite to truth. It's about challenging the business truths that sabotage success.

It's about shifting the way that you think about the myths that you've been told in business so that you may discover new possibilities.

The four common myths that you may have been told:

Myth #1: Be More Decisive
Myth #2: Be More Proactive
Myth #3: Be More Positive
Myth #4: Be More Present

How MVPs shift their thinking about these myths:

Shift #1: Be More Decisive...But Re-Decide When
  It's Not Working
Shift #2: Be More Proactive...Once The Original Job Is Done
Shift #3: Be More Positive...Or Just Positive Enough
Shift #4: Be More Present...Unless The Present Moment Stinks

Being an MVP is about being praiseworthy in whatever areas of your life you implement the ideas presented in this book. It's about not taking things at face value. It's about shifting your mindset about the myths that may be holding you back, shifting your thinking about the myths that sound good on paper but lose steam in reality.

When you practice shifting your thinking about the myths as they relate to hiring, you will be on the lookout for future MVPs of the company, not just a body to fill a role.

When you utilize the suggestions about shifting your thinking about the myths surrounding leading or managing a team, you will quickly assess the soft skills that will make or break the success of your team.

When you shift your thinking about the myths with customers and clients, you will be more attractive to do business with, and your experience of doing business with these clients and customers will improve.

Myth Shift addresses more things that we want more of from our staff and from ourselves. But wait, there's more...

In order for MVPs to play to their full potential and win, the environment throughout the rest of the organization must be deliberately designed to support them. In the Appendix, business leaders and managers will discover the four things that MVPs want more of from their leaders, bosses, managers, and owners. And (spoiler alert) it has nothing to do with money.

Before you get too far into this book, I invite you to consider two game-changing questions:

1. If everyone in my organization was worthy of receiving the MVP award, what would be possible for the organization as a whole? Said another way, if everyone was an MVP player, we could accomplish _____.

2. If we were able to achieve _____, how would I feel? If everyone was an MVP player and we could accomplish _____, I would feel _____.

With the answers to these two questions in mind, whether you are the CEO, the company barista, a salesperson, or sorting mail, you may create new possibilities for yourself and your organization by shifting your view about business myths.

When I'm invited to speak to a group, whether I'm the keynote speaker kicking off a large conference or the event is a more moderate executive off-site meeting where we dive deeper into the myths that need shifting, I typically start by challenging the participants with two statements. Below is some dialogue from a recent gathering with a group of executives:

Merit: If everyone was an MVP player, we would be able to

_____.

David: Exceed every goal and deliver epic customer service.

Steven: Be respected in the community.

Tamara: Reach our sales goals with ease.

Merit: And if you exceeded every goal, delivered epic customer service, were respected in the community, and reached your sales goals with ease, you would feel _____.

David: Blessed and appreciative.

Steven: Relaxed.

Tamara: Successful and proud to manage a team of people like that.

You might be wondering why this topic matters to me enough to speak about, write about, and consult with organizations about. Growing people (not in the Petri dish sense of the word) in terms of growing their confidence, growing their skills, and growing what they perceive is possible for themselves is a central theme in this book.

Why should companies care about growing people? Because the smartest business leaders know that by growing people you grow profits. With an organization full of MVPs, it's easier to attract and recruit more MVPs. MVPs are more engaged in their jobs and are more likely to stay with a company longer, which impacts a company's attrition rate and the bottom line.

With an organization full of MVPs, it's easier to attract and keep more and better clients and customers. With an organization full of MVPs, it's easier to increase market share, innovate, and make a difference.

In a sense, possibly because my name means worthy of praise, I've always known that shining the light on what it takes to earn acknowledgment would be my life's work.

MVPS are always on the lookout for myths to shift. MVPs implement the ideas presented in this book every day, not just when someone is watching them. They are consistent because they are always watching themselves. Being an MVP matters to them. Like the tree that may or may not make a sound in the forest if nobody is around to hear it fall, MVPs unfailingly take the actions, have the mindset, and have the perspective of an MVP, regardless of whether the boss is around to see or hear them.

Greg was on the operations side of a large manufacturing company and was responsible for bringing a new guy on board. A week after the new guy started, Greg noticed that any time their boss was walking around the plant, the new guy stood and smiled as he worked. As soon as the manager left the building, he went back to slouching. It was like he was putting on a show for the manager.

Greg questioned the new guy about what he had observed.

The new guy responded, "The only time you have to look like you enjoy what you're doing is when the boss is watching."

As luck would have it, just as the new guy shared his wisdom with Greg, the manager appeared in the doorway. For a more dramatic ending to the story, it would be fun to tell you that the new guy was fired on the spot, but what actually happened was that the manager recognized the teachable moment for everyone, not just the clearly misled new guy.

As the legend goes, Michael Jordan practiced free throws for thirty extra minutes after practice every day, but not because the coach was watching. He did it because he knew that everybody else wasn't doing it and that it would give him the edge. He did it because of how it made him feel and perform in his role as an elite basketball player. Of course, he didn't just do the extra credit, he layered it on top of doing the rest of his job exceptionally well.

Selectively performing at the MVP level only when you have an audience to impress won't make you a real MVP. The magic is in the consistent application of the concepts outlined in this book, day in and day out.

Fight the methodology, and you might never become the MVP that you could be or inspire others around you to become MVPs. You may see and hear friends and co-workers playing small and know that that is enough for them, but not for you. Don't let your friends suck you into playing a diminished game.

Years ago, when I worked in a sales and sales management training company, our training center could support forty clients comfortably. As we reached capacity, the other trainers slowed down their selling efforts. My goal was to serve more people, not just the number of people who fit nicely into the four walls of the office.

If I had let them, the other trainers in the office would have drawn me into their little game. I was not interested in playing small, so I continued to sell and add more classes to the schedule. I shaped a new possibility for the entire organization because I made a new decision that served me better, was proactive where it mattered, was just positive enough, and I chose my perspective of the present moment carefully.

But the business success came at a cost. While I was increasing business, the other trainers shunned me. I didn't get invitations to go to lunch or out for drinks after work. As I look back on that time, from a different perspective, I realize that I outgrew those relationships. The work that I was doing was making these trainers look bad, so to make themselves feel better, they excluded and ridiculed me.

Playing small was of no interest to me, and shifting their thinking about the myths about being more decisive, more proactive, more positive, and more present was of no interest to them. They were happy with the level of success that the company had achieved. They wanted me to lower my expectations to meet our current results rather than do what was necessary to modify their behaviors to meet our future expectations.

Why do people stop thinking BIG? Why do people stop taking action toward their dreams and goals? Why do people stop pushing themselves? Why don't people engage in MVP-level performance at work every day?

Have people stopped sharing original ideas to help grow your company? Have people stopped recommending innovative products and services? Have they stopped improving processes, saving money, or protecting company resources? Have you, the person holding this book, stopped dreaming of new possibilities?

When you or your team stop thinking about what could be possible, does that cost you money, market share, time, or energy? Do those added costs impact your sense of satisfaction? Do you or the people who work for you feel overwhelmed, frustrated, out of balance, or disengaged?

If you are on the planet in this game of life long enough, you will experience tough times. When the economy takes a downturn, so do our attitudes, beliefs, and outlook. It's hard to stay positive and upbeat when surrounded by so much negativity. It is harder to see what could be possible on the other side of the rainbow when the storm clouds are all that you can see now.

For years I taught a class on the topic of who you are is not what you do, the basic idea being that how we feel about ourselves should not depend upon a good or bad result at work.

I remember coming home from teaching that class one time and talking to my husband. "I'm so depressed."

"Why?"

"I didn't explain the notion of separating yourself from your role at work very well in class tonight."

He laughed out loud. I didn't get the joke at the time.

Even teaching the class didn't make the principle any easier to execute in real life.

It's time for the turnaround. It's time to focus on earning acknowledgment so that you feel more engaged at work, lead a more dynamic team, accomplish your goals, and generate amazing possibilities for your life as an MVP. It's a crucial concept, but not one easily put into practice in the world of business.

Don't let the marketplace dictate your possibilities. Flex your mindset-shifting muscles as outlined in this book and be in control of possibility creation.

People who actively shift their thinking about these myths find new possibilities for their careers and their lives. They are MVPs in all areas of their lives.

The process of igniting the MVP in you, in all of us, is daunting, but my vision is to spark MVP ways of being in people and in teams in organizations, one person at a time. No matter who you are, what you do, where you live, how much money you do or don't have, the state of your health, your religion, your lifestyle, or your political choices, you may make use of the ideas in this book and forge new possibilities for your life and your work.

If you are tired of the status quo and are ready to feel good about what you might discover, you are an MVP waiting to emerge. If you are fed up with doing all that you are doing just to get by and are ready to allow yourself to dream again about what you may do with your life, you are an MVP at heart. If you have been unclear about what you want or unsure that you could make it happen, but you are willing to trust that you may do something more, you have what it takes to be an MVP.

MVPs are not satisfied with the status quo. The status quo is suffocating. Comfort zones kill creativity. MVPs know that more is possible, and though many of them may go into hibernation when the economy goes south, they don't stay there for long.

This book is for anyone who is not willing to wait for the latest statistics about the economy, the unemployment rate, or consumer spending to tell them that all is well, or can be soon. This book is for all of the entrepreneurs, business leaders, salespeople, innovators, professionals, and other working people who have ideas and goals that they know will improve their lives and the lives of others, and they are not going to wait for conditions to be perfect in the world to launch their dreams.

This book is for people who know that the promise is there but have not yet been able to put the puzzle together to move toward worthier possibilities.

Little did I know when my parents named me Merit that it would set me on a journey to discover for myself and then teach others the path to becoming worthy of praise.

It kind of makes me wonder what my life's work would have been if my parents had named me Jill...

Be More Decisive

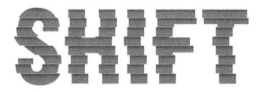

But Re-Decide
When It's Not Working

PART I

Myth #1

Be More Decisive

Definiteness of decision always requires courage, sometimes very great courage. The fifty-six men who signed the Declaration of Independence staked their lives on the decision to affix their signatures to that document.
~ Napoleon Hill, *Think and Grow Rich*

You've likely been told that making a decision is a good thing and that once you make a decision you should stick with it, be committed to it. Right? Well, what if that decision was a bad one that ultimately could hurt you? Is it still best to stick with it because it was the original decision?

That we need to be more decisive is myth #1. Have you ever made a snap decision or a decision under pressure just to prove that you could be decisive? I have. It didn't turn out well. There are times when being decisive is a strength, but there are also times when it's valuable to take another look at the decisions you've made and make an adjustment.

It may have been a strange choice to begin this part of the book with a quote about the men who made a monumental decision and signed the Declaration of Independence. I want to talk about the importance of making a decision but also introduce the concept of *re-deciding* when the decision that you first made is not working out as planned. Let me say, for the record, that I'm not suggesting that we re-decide the Declaration of Independence, the Constitution, or the Bill of Rights!

I suppose that the founding fathers of the United States of America in a sense re-decided how they wanted to be governed because the system under which England operated wasn't working for them any longer.

You have the ability to do the same thing. Maybe it's something basic like the route you take commuting to work that is no longer working for you and needs to be re-decided. Maybe it's the game-plan that you put together to reach your business goals that isn't producing the results that you desire that needs to be re-decided. Maybe it's the relationships with colleagues who do nothing but complain that needs to be re-decided.

The men who devised the structure of a new country had choices. They didn't want more of the same, they wanted something better. To this day, more than two hundred years later, these men are still worthy of praise in the eyes of Americans and much of the world. They are true MVPs. They challenged all kinds of myths and shifted their mindset about what is possible to meet their new vision.

I'm not particular about how you get to MVP status. There is truth to the old wisdom of Napoleon Hill who also said, *Whatever the mind of man can conceive and believe, it can achieve.* I've seen numerous times where a *fake it 'til you make it* or an *act as if* attitude led to belief and more action.

By the time a thought becomes conscious to you, it's likely been in your subconscious for a while, though you didn't know it. Once it is a conscious thought, you get to choose what to believe that will serve you best.

It is imperative to distinguish a particular aspect of shifting your thinking about myths that will allow you to make the necessary adjustments in your ways of being and still keep your ego happy.

Here is the rule that MVPs live by: Being more decisive, as in sticking with a decision just because you already decided it, is not always the best thing to do. Consider that there is an enormous difference between *re-deciding* something versus *changing your mind*. Hang with me...

Okay, I was going to go on and on, but I re-decided, and I'll end this section here.

Re-Deciding Versus Changing Your Mind

I feel I change my mind all the time.
And I sort of feel that's your responsibility
as a person, as a human being—to constantly be updating
your positions on as many things as possible.
And if you don't contradict yourself on a regular basis,
then you're not thinking.
~ Malcolm Gladwell

You must be comfortable with the idea of re-deciding before we attack the business wisdom that we've been told was truth and shift the myths.

Let's take an example. In the reality show, *The Biggest Loser,* contestants compete with each other to see who can lose the highest percentage of body fat each week for thirteen weeks.

The television show is a hit because people may see with their own eyes what can happen when people believe that more (or in this case *less*) is possible for themselves.

Some contestants have hit rock bottom. They are out of shape, massively overweight, and unhealthy. What they gain from the show is clarity about what they want; a healthy, strong body; a lower number on the scale; and less body fat as a percentage of their total weight.

They spend countless hours in the gym with professional trainers to rid their bodies of excess fat. They learn new strategies for healthy eating. They stand on a scale on national television. I'm sure that they didn't believe that these things were possible before being on the show.

What I like most about the program is that there are moments when you see something shift in the contestants, when they move from thinking that they could possibly lose weight to the unwavering commitment to follow the program, do whatever it takes, and get their desired result. In that moment they have re-decided a long-standing belief that they could not lose weight.

They didn't just change their mind to lose weight this time. It was more masterful than that. They had new information, new tools and trainers, not to mention the pressure of a nationally televised weigh-in.

With that re-decision, new possibilities are awakened within them. With the internal changes come the external results.

Some contestants may not believe that they can lose the weight until they start seeing the pounds come off. For them, action came first, and really believing in a new possibility was the byproduct of that successful action.

The danger in the action-before-the-belief equation is that if the action isn't successful, it will further cement the belief that your ego wants to keep intact. Your ego says I told you so. You can't lose weight! This self-limiting belief makes life easier for the ego, which thinks that you are perfect just the way you are, even if you have a higher risk of heart attack. Thanks a lot, ego.

Give your ego a vacation, and re-decide beliefs that were given to you or that no longer serve you.

As long as the contestants see themselves as an obese person who struggles with weight, they will make decisions to support that belief and justify their results (or lack thereof). When they believe that they can overcome their weight challenges, their actions in the gym are supercharged. Their bodies begin working in concert with their minds, and that's where the magic lives.

What the trainers on the show give the contestants is an optimistic outlook that they can do it, while also providing them with a healthy side dish of reality-check. Then the trainers provoke action. Measuring and tracking the contestants' progress along the way, the trainers help the contestants see the results of the actions, and this helps them believe that they can do it. They keep on keeping on, and by the end of the television season, the contestants have collectively lost hundreds and hundreds of pounds.

Contestants on the show are in action long before their new belief about what is possible really kicks in. Yes, it could be the formula for the TV show, but the pattern is that the contestants think that they might lose weight, they take action in the gym, and they have some success. Just when they start to truly believe that they can accomplish their goal, a setback challenges their commitment and belief.

The contestants overcome the challenges, both in mind and body, and then it happens. Their level of belief comes to match their level of action, and they get the results they've always wanted.

What you see on TV is what happens when people re-decide what is possible.

In my work as a business development coach and consultant, my primary goal is to let my clients know, when they first hire me, that I know more about what is possible for them than they do. It's exactly what the trainers on the TV show do for the people on their team who want to lose weight.

Every woman knows (and reminds the men in her life) that it is a woman's prerogative to change her mind. My husband has grown tired of this female predilection. And then I discovered the potency of *re-deciding*.

Permission changes everything. You need to give yourself permission to re-decide. That is impressive. When you make a decision and affirm it to the world, you are stuck with it. There is social pressure when you make a goal public. Sometimes this is a good thing and helpful in keeping you committed to taking the actions that are necessary to reach the goal.

But, there is one tiny problem with this. What if you get new information that changes your thinking? Do you still have to move forward with your original decision just because you already decided it and announced it to the world? After all, you don't want to be known as someone who can't make a decision, do you?

Try this on for size. Giving yourself permission to re-decide based on new information or a change in core values is okay. There is energy in re-deciding that is not available to you when you change your mind at the drop of a hat. Changing your mind often may be seen as wimpy and wishy-washy. We see this frequently in the political arena. Politicians have been called flip-floppers. This is not a good look for someone on the path to becoming the MVP of their organization...or the President of the United States.

Our thoughts determine our reality. We have the ability to choose our thoughts. Decisions come after thoughts. You decide based on your beliefs. You believe what you think. Carefully choosing your thoughts and beliefs is the basis of all good decision-making.

If you change your thinking based on new data, that is cause to modify your beliefs, but your ego likes to hold on firmly to beliefs, and that makes it difficult to make a different decision.

Remember when everyone thought the world was flat? Well, of course you don't remember it, but you remember hearing about it. A whole lot of people had to re-decide that belief when new information became available. I'm pretty sure that nobody considered these re-deciders weak flip-floppers.

One primary belief that you may hold that you might wish to consider is this: Do you believe that the world is basically good? Or do you believe that the universe is out to get you? If you think that the world is a decent place, then all of your decisions will line up to support that key belief. If you believe that the world is an evil place where people or situations are out to get you, then all of your decisions will be based on that fundamental belief.

You will go to extraordinary lengths to prove to yourself and everyone around you that what you believe is the truth. Well, you don't do that, but your ego does! Your ego will fight pretty hard to be right no matter what the cost. More blood has been shed over being right than anything else in history. Sure, it looks like a fight over land, money, religion, politics, or something else, but at the core it's about proving that you, or your side, is right. It hardly seems worth it to me, though my ego doesn't always see it that way.

Decisions to do something or not to do something will be in alignment with your basic beliefs.

As a young voter, and I'm not proud of this, I voted for the person my parents liked, or, if I happened to be mad at them, I voted another way. (A superb strategy for selecting the leader of the free world, huh!). As I got older, I re-decided this voting decision based on new information that I sought out. Human beings don't do enough of that, thinking for themselves, I mean.

Re-deciding beliefs is an ongoing process. Opportunities will continue to come your way that may test your new beliefs. There is nothing wrong with that. Embrace those opportunities, as they will strengthen your new beliefs.

With a clear understanding of your beliefs, you may inventory those beliefs and decide which ones serve you in a positive way and which ones it would be best to re-decide. While we vigorously choose some of our beliefs, many are inherited.

When I started my own sales training business, I created the title Chief Belief Officer for myself because my primary role and responsibility was to believe in what was truly possible for my clients before they believed it themselves. I explained that all they had to do was believe in my ability to see more for them and trust the process to get them there.

It was easier for them to believe in my ability to see possibilities for them than it was to believe in the possibilities for themselves. Eventually my clients started to shift their beliefs about what was possible for them, and new belief patterns were put into place.

We could all use a Chief Belief Officer in our lives. But belief alone won't make you an MVP. You can't just wake up and say *from now on I believe that more is possible* and have an MVP trophy on your desk by noon. Life doesn't work that way.

You must be more deliberate. You must be in constant motion. You must allow yourself to re-decide when it is appropriate.

The question then becomes, does belief follow action, or does action follow belief? Do you do something because you believe that more is possible, or does the belief spur the action?

I have had experiences where the belief precedes manifestation. In other words, because of my belief that it was possible, I made it so. I have also experienced times when the belief wasn't strong enough to rely on, so I took action. Through consistent action I experienced a shift in my belief about what was possible, and in the end, because of the action, the goal was achieved, and along with this my beliefs were re-decided.

Did you know that when General George Washington was appointed to lead the army of rebels fighting the British for freedom, he didn't believe that he had the chops to get the job done? According to Bill O'Reilly's book, *Legends and Lies*, Washington was uncertain about his abilities as a General, but he never let his men see his doubt.

I was stunned to learn that the person who became the first President of the United States and whose face is on the one-dollar bill had to fake it till he made it. He had to re-decide his beliefs and actions because his very life, and the future of a country, depended on it.

Some of us need the certainty of belief before taking any action. Others need to be in action before they can believe that something can happen. Know your strategy, and be willing to re-decide it when necessary.

Amber had been working as an inside sales rep and had recently accepted a promotion to outside sales. She loved the company she worked for and was concerned about moving into a new role and not being prepared to succeed in that position.

The first thing we did was to assess her level of effort and positive outlook. Then we assessed whether the environment was set up for her to be successful in her new role. Did she have the tools to be successful? Did she have opportunities to fit in with her new team? Would she have a chance to do work that mattered to her? Were there opportunities for her good work to be appreciated?

Unfortunately, this was the first time that the company had moved someone from inside sales to outside sales, and the processes and tools were not in place for her to do well. She had always wanted to be in outside sales, but she wanted to be smart about it.

She re-decided the acceptance of the promotion and stayed in her current role in inside sales. While she did her job, she groomed herself for the outside sales position. She put herself through sales training and got to know the sales team. She also identified a niche that was important to her that was not being filled by the current salesforce.

Within twelve months, she was ready to walk into the outside sales role with confidence, and within two years she was the MVP of the organization. She had an MVP mindset before she started in outside sales. She was prepared for success in a way that she would not have been had she taken the position when it was initially offered to her.

Amber could have taken the position in spite of the realities of the situation just because it was the path that she was on and because it was what there was to do, but it would not have served her well. She could have taken on the new role simply because it was a promotion and just accepted the fallacy that any promotion is a good promotion. She didn't change her mind about the overall goal, she re-decided the best path to get herself there.

Re-deciding what you want based on your core values and accurate data is a gift.

It's time to draw a line in the sand about what behaviors, attitudes, and results are right for you. It is time to draw a line in the sand about what you and your team are truly capable of and want to accomplish. It's time to re-decide what is keeping you from seeing new possibilities for yourself and your organization.

Sometimes when we think about how we sell or market certain products or services, we realize that over time decisions made previously have lost their luster. That's when you know it's time to re-decide.

Years ago, The Pony Express was the best way to deliver a message quickly. As more tools, technology, and options became available, it would have been a mistake not to have re-decided the best way to send a message.

Re-deciding based upon new options and knowledge available is a clever thing to do. Sticking with a decision just because you made it and professed it to the world before becoming aware of new information is silly.

Another successful salesperson whom I coached was offered a promotion to be the sales manager. He thought that this was what he wanted, so he accepted the position. Within ninety days, he knew that he had made the wrong decision. He loved the freedom and the autonomy of outside sales but disliked the manager meetings, the paperwork, and the reporting required of him in this role. Rather than being miserable in this new job, he re-decided his desires, had a straightforward conversation with his boss, and went back to his job in outside sales, with zero regrets.

When I was 14 years old, I must have watched the movie *Sixteen Candles* dozens of times. That was when I *decided* that I would have two children, and older boy with a younger sister. My son's name would be Jake (like the gorgeous character, Jake Ryan, in the movie). Later, when I was about 20 years old, I decided on my daughter's name because I had fallen in love with Sydney, Australia. Her name would be Sydney.

Fast-forward to age 28, when I met my dream man, David. We talked about children, and I told him my master plan, because I had already decided to have two children and name them Jake and Sydney.

He had reservations about having two children. "We'll see how the first one goes..."

I was sure that I heard him correctly. "The first one will be fantabulous, and I'll be super excited for another!"

(Later you'll learn that that was my Pollyanna optimistic side talking, but that won't make sense to you until Chapter 7).

After a few years of marriage we decided to start our family. I knew that my plan was working perfectly when my son was born. It will not surprise you to learn that we named him Jake. After all, I was committed to a decision that I had made public a mere 19 years before.

It wasn't until Jake was 3 years old, playing on the playground with three other kids, that I regretted my naming decision. Of the four kids on the playground that day, three of them were named Jake, and the fourth was a girl. Growing up with a unique name like Merit, I was certain that I wanted my son to have a more common name, but maybe I overachieved when it comes to the prevalence of the name Jake.

A year later, Dave and I started talking about having a second child, but he was not keen on the idea.

I was faced with a monster decision.

I loved my husband and my son, but I desperately wanted another child. I unconsciously started sabotaging my marriage. Whenever

Dave wanted to be with Jake, I snapped at him as if he didn't have the right to enjoy this beautiful baby boy because he didn't want another child. This impacted our marriage, and I realized that I was destroying the family that I did have because of the fantasy family that I had decided I would have back when I was 14.

Decision time, or rather, re-decision time. I could make my current family miserable because it wouldn't ever be my original picture of my family, or I could re-decide to enjoy every millisecond of time with my husband and my son and the lovely family that we are and be happy with life as it is.

Sometimes life doesn't turn out as we planned it. I'm sure you have a story of your own that demonstrates the truth in that statement. Life sometimes makes decisions for us, and they are not the same decisions that we would make for ourselves.

That's re-decision time. We are deceived if we believe that happiness is only achieved when we get what we thought we wanted in the exact form in which we wanted it. Another myth.

Funny, the other players in our lives never got the advance copy of the life script that we carefully crafted for them.

Embrace re-deciding. If you look at it as giving in or giving up, you will be filled with regret, and those nasty feelings lead to actions that may be even more damaging. If you embrace the concept of re-deciding based on new information, you have adopted a much more savvy position and one that your ego may live with happily.

Okay, let's apply the principle of re-deciding to growing a business. When the economy took a downturn in 2008, many of my clients had to re-decide how they would perform in their roles. In the heyday just two years earlier, businesses were successful in spite of sloppy sales techniques and minimal marketing endeavors.

When it became clear that the marketplace was changing, it was time for business people to get clarity around the behaviors that it would take to grow the business in that economy. They had to re-decide their day-to-day activities.

Some salespeople took the opportunity to re-decide their career in sales altogether. Some re-decided the company where they wanted to work. Some had to re-decide *after* they were let go.

In the training area of my business, I noticed a change in client behavior. For years I ran a weekly class in my training center, and classes were always full. When my family moved to Denver, Colorado, in 2008 (because we love the outdoors...not because of marijuana), I planned to set up the same type of business model that I had used in Chicago. I built the same training calendar and decided to deliver the material in the same way that I had so successfully in Chicago for more than ten years.

It didn't take me long to discover that the marketplace was different in Denver. In Chicago, it was not unusual to have to drive an hour or more to get to your destination. The expectation was that a commute time of an hour was par for the course. In Denver, where lifestyle trumps just about everything else, a twenty-minute drive for a business activity was considered out of the way (ask anyone from Denver, and they will tell you that I'm not exaggerating). Denver folks think nothing of driving three hours to ski, hike, or bike, but business was another story.

That piece of information dramatically limited the radius of possible clients for me. I could have fought the reality of the situation, but instead I re-decided how I would deliver training and implemented instead a two-day intensive program with a full year of weekly teleseminars for reinforcement and support coaching.

This re-decision allowed me to expand my reach way beyond the Denver market. I could easily do business with people from across the country because it was not a big deal for them to fly into Denver for two days of training.

I didn't re-decide about the business I was in, I just re-decided how I ran the business I loved. Without real data, it's harder to make new decisions. Ignoring the reality and sticking to a plan or goal that you know is no longer working is insanity. MVPs don't do that, especially when it's so easy to shift their mindset and find a way to make it work.

The falsehood in this case was that I could duplicate the exact same business in a different city, in a different economic environment, and with a different set of personal priorities than I had when I started the original company in 1998. The shift in my thinking was that I could indeed duplicate the results I wanted, but I didn't have to utilize the same strategy to achieve those results.

I don't consider myself a failure for not being able to make an in-person weekly class model a success in the Denver market, I consider myself highly in-tune to the needs of my prospects, my clients, myself, and my family. The new decision to deliver training in a different way made it easier for companies to work with me and easier for salespeople to get the reinforcement they needed, even if they had to be on the road themselves.

This re-decision also made it easier for me to enjoy the Colorado lifestyle! It was a win-win-win all the way around.

In 1994 and 1995, I backpacked around the world on my own. Many backpackers whom I met felt, as I did, as if they were on the hamster wheel of life. The typical path after graduating from college is to get a job, work, date people in order to find the one, get married, have a baby, buy a new home, move to the suburbs, put up the white picket fence, commute to work on the train or in traffic, get a promotion, have baby number two, get a dog, and, well, you get where I'm going.

Every backpacker I met had decided to jump off of that hamster wheel onto a different wheel, the wheel of adventure travel, and give that wheel a few spins. Sure, many would eventually bounce off of the exciting wheel and vault back onto the traditional wheel, as I did, but it was a choice.

First, these folks decided on the conventional path. Then they re-decided based on new information and their current core values. For me, I'm forever grateful that I originally jumped off of the hamster wheel and had a wondrous adventure. I met travelers who had been on the road for years. Though I considered that type of lifestyle, it ultimately wasn't for me, so I re-decided and chose to return to my more typical American journey.

Every now and then I quiz myself, as all MVPs do, "What more is possible beyond the confines of the wheel that I am on right now?"

Without the distinction between re-deciding and changing our mind, we often stick to our stated goals or build up a stockpile of justifiable excuses about why we are being blocked from accomplishing our goals. Resistance kills possibilities. Stop it. You now have permission to re-decide anything that no longer serves you as long as you are making the re-decision based on new information and checking in with your current core values.

Re-deciding a goal because you can't see a path to get you there or it seems too much of a stretch is a cop out. I am not advocating adjusting your goals downward to meet your current situation. I'm advocating re-deciding goals and game-plans that are no longer the answer to creating new possibilities and opportunities in your life.

No matter what the scenario, if you re-decide prior to an event, because of it, or after the event, the point is that you always have a choice in the matter. If things happen to you and you have no say in them, you will be a victim, and you will never be considered an MVP.

Only when you feel powerful can you be in control of your own destiny. Only when you are in control of your own destiny can you grow your sales, your career, or yourself. You will limit your possibilities for today and the future if you cling to the self-limiting belief that bad things happen to you.

Things happen. You decide if you are going to cry about it or make it work for you in the end. (There is nothing wrong with a little crying, just have a strategy to rebound. More about that in Chapter 11.)

What do you need to re-decide about how you do your business? Who you do business with? How you package your services and products? What's next for your career? How you hire or what an MVP looks like during an interview? How you prepare new hires for long-term success?

Now that we've got the definition of re-deciding all sorted out, there's one last detail that we need to cover before we take a look at the other common myths in business that are holding you back from MVP status...

- Go back in time and write down your top three to five core values that drove your decisions ten years ago.

- From the perspective of today, write down your top three to five core values. Did they change?

- Consider a recent decision you made. Did you think about old values or more recent values?

- If you are making decisions today based on values from the past, it's time for a shift in thinking.

- The next time you have a decision to make, think about whether you will get more or less of what you value now by making the decision in a particular way.

- Evaluate a decision that you made some time ago. Compare this decision to your current core values. If you would not make the same decision today, consider re-deciding the decision.

2

The Opposite Of Re-Deciding Is Resistance

*I may be wrong in regard to any or all of them; but holding it
a sound maxim, that it is better to be only sometimes right,
than at all times wrong, so soon as I discover my opinions
to be erroneous, I shall be ready to renounce them.*
~ Abraham Lincoln, Speeches and Writing, 1832 through 1858

Over the years I have taught goal-setting in a variety of formats. Sometimes I have used a fill-in-the-blank template with soft music playing in the background and lots of silent moments for students to think and write. Other times the class has been rowdy, and I turn on some swing music and provide lots of magazines, scissors, glue sticks, and poster boards for participants to design visions of their desires. Of course, there were countless private coaching sessions where my clients and I discussed their goals and dreams and then constructed the action plans to get them to where they wanted to go.

Most of my clients over the years have set goals during our work together at some point. Some have come to me with goals that they have had for a number of years. True, some just needed a good plan and a coach to hold them accountable for doing the activities, but what I found most interesting was their own resistance. *The opposite of re-deciding is resistance.*

When you set a goal, but it no longer serves you, you have two choices:

1. Re-decide the original goal so that it now works for you.
2. Resist re-deciding, and try to force completion of your goal.

My husband, David, is going through this very issue right now as I write this book. He set his goal to be a real estate developer, one who can deliver a healthy return for his investors, fix and flip old homes to please buyers, and build our retirement fund.

When he started the business, our son hadn't yet been born, and David's core values were fun, love, and financial abundance. I'm proud to say that he is accomplishing his goals. The problem is that while he was building his real estate empire in Chicago, we moved to Denver, and now his work requires him to be away from his family more than he would like.

It has been eight years and counting. He is still traveling back and forth from Denver to Chicago, between home and work. *On some level he is resisting re-deciding.*

People who know him know that it's time for him to re-decide. According to a February 2016 article on Realtor.com, Denver is number nine on a list of the top twenty hottest U.S. real estate markets. Chicago didn't even make the list. It sure seems odd that he's resistant to moving his business to Denver.

It's not unusual to resist change. That's just part of being human.

David is influential in Chicago. He's got a team in Chicago. He knows the Chicago market. His investors are in Chicago. It's easy to do what he's doing. Sometimes it's easier to resist than it is to re-decide.

With re-decision, he would be required to take action, re-build a business, and learn a new market, among other things. He doesn't necessarily have to re-decide doing real estate. He may not even have to stop doing it in Chicago, but he may have to re-decide how he operates the business, how much he wants or is able to do on his own, and how he uses technology to assist him. He may have to talk to the current happy investors about doing projects in Denver rather than in Chicago or doing some commercial work rather than residential.

The changes will be easier once he re-decides based upon his current true values, which are fun, love, and family. Don't get me wrong, financial abundance is still on the radar screen, which is probably why it's easy to continue to resist re-deciding, but given the choice between money and family, it's not as uncomplicated a choice as it once was.

Running a Chicago real estate development firm was not a bad original goal or one that he couldn't achieve, it's just that compared to his current lifestyle, the achievement of the goal is no longer enough. It's not bad or wrong to continue as is, but he is starting to resent having to travel and miss out on family time.

When resistance turns into resentment, it is time to re-decide.

If the folks at 3M had been stuck (no pun intended) on the idea of inventing the glue that would stick to things forever, they might have missed the potential of the Post-It note. Perhaps they still had the goal of inventing the forever glue, but they recognized a new possibility along the way, and based on the number of Post-It notes that I alone have purchased, it has served them well. They didn't resist the re-decision, and the company made millions of dollars as a result.

Several years ago one of the companies for which I was doing training and consulting work was purchased by another company. As is the standard practice in any merger or acquisition scenario, the two companies had to blend their people, processes, practices, and culture into one.

Ideally, each company would select the best of its own company and learn from the other company. In reality, it doesn't work that way as often as it should, and one company openly takes over and mandates to the other how it's going to be from now on. That leaves people with a choice, resist the mandate or re-decide how they will work within the new structure.

Companies, like people, may have egos. After all, a company is the sum total of all of the egos of its leadership team. That may be both good and bad, depending on the individuals involved.

If a company resists change simply for the sake of resisting, well, this could be bad. If a company recognizes change and looks deeper into the possible outcomes of the change, with a sense of perspective (which we will talk about in more detail in Chapter 10), change may be good.

Company leaders who consider the option of re-deciding versus resisting are the strongest leaders around.

What are you resisting re-deciding? What is it costing you personally, professionally, financially, and emotionally by resisting? What would be available to you, as a possibility, if you re-decided a specific area that you have been resisting?

Okay. Now you are ready to apply another mindset shift to the next myth and to open your mind to more possibilities in your work and in your life.

MVPs don't base their present and future actions on goals from the past. They assess current core values and re-decide the beliefs and actions necessary to accomplish an updated version of their life and work objectives. This is not always easy on the ego, but it does take some proactive movement forward. So let's move on to *Part II, Myth #2... Be More Proactive.*

SHIFT STARTERS

We saw these questions in the chapter, but they are highlighted here to emphasize the importance of considering their impact. We aren't going to write anything down because we don't want a paper trail, but on your own, gauge where you may be resisting making a re-decision.

This can be tough stuff. You will be stuck with business myths that will sabotage your success until you are willing and able to address these questions:

- What are you resisting re-deciding?

- What is it costing you personally, professionally, financially, and emotionally by resisting?

- What would be available to you, as a possibility, if you re-decided a specific area that you have been resisting?

Be More Proactive

**Once The Original
Job Is Done**

PART II

Myth #2

Be More Proactive

*People who end up with the good jobs are the proactive ones
who are solutions to problems, not problems themselves,
who seize the initiative to do whatever is necessary,
consistent with correct principles, to get the job done.*
~ Stephen R. Covey, *The 7 Habits of Highly Effective People:
Powerful Lessons in Personal Change*

Okay, strap yourself in, I'm about to challenge a myth that you have probably been praised for believing and following. In fact, you could argue that the quote above is in support of being more proactive so why the heck am I telling you that being more proactive is a business myth that I am here to bust?

First of all, let me be crystal clear. I am not in any way saying that you should not be proactive. Huh? The myth to be busted is *be more proactive* and I'm still telling you to be proactive? Time to read another less contradictory book, right? Wrong. This book is about the slight shifts in thinking and actions that MVPs demonstrate consistently.

There are two ways of looking at being proactive. If you are proactively solving problems directly related to your number one responsibility, splendid. Skip ahead to Myth #3. The reason I'm suggesting that *be more proactive* is a myth is because it is misunderstood. If you are being proactive in areas that are unrelated to your most important job then you are fooling yourself. You think that you are an

MVP because you are always running around helping others and wearing the busy badge of honor, but you may actually be creating extra work for your colleagues if your number one accountability is overlooked.

What is important is the context and timing of your proactive behavior. Here's the rule that MVPs live by: Being more proactive, as in looking around for other things to do, is only a good thing when the original task is complete.

Where people get mixed up is when they haven't done their most important work before they start looking around for other ways to be helpful. MVPs simply don't do that. MVPs focus on their primary job, they get it done on time, they do it well and then they proactively identify other ways to contribute.

When this slight distinction is left out of the conversation about the value of being proactive, people get it wrong, and being proactive doesn't get them any closer to MVP status. In fact, people who consider themselves to be proactive end up confused and disgruntled when they don't get recognized for going the extra mile. In their minds they are going above and beyond, but in reality, they've done extra work while their primary job is incomplete, inaccurate, ineffective, or just plain insufficient.

First, let's consider the merits (sorry, couldn't help it) of being proactive. Then we will consider the barriers to being more proactive. Remember, the shift in thinking about the being more proactive myth is that looking around for other things to do is only a good thing when the original task is complete (more on that concept in Chapter 6).

Andrea was an Executive Assistant to the owner of a busy manufacturer distribution company. The owner was expecting an urgent FedEx delivery on a Tuesday, and Andrea would be the only person in the office to receive it. As Andrea was leaving for work Tuesday morning, her car wouldn't start.

Consequently, she made three phone calls, in this order: she called FedEx to make sure that the package could be held at a facility where she could pick it up later in the day, she called a mechanic, and then she called her boss to let him know why she would be working from home and that she'd already made arrangements to pick up the package that he was expecting.

What a gift to have someone working for you who doesn't dump problems back into your lap. Andrea could have called her boss and told him that her car wouldn't start, that she couldn't make it to work, and made the FedEx package the boss's problem to deal with. Not a nifty move if you want to be considered an MVP. Fortunately for Andrea, she is a prime example of someone who is proactive in a good way.

Over the years, much of my consulting work has been focused on preparing companies acquiring large numbers of new employees to get these newcomers up to speed quickly in their new roles. Often, hiring managers want to hire individuals who will hit the ground running, predominantly because they don't have the time or the training capabilities to assist the new hire. If they can bring someone on who already knows what to do, their perception is that life will be easier. While it may be less effort to hire someone who walks in the door with some skills and industry experience to build upon, the person whom these managers really want is someone who is proactive when it comes to getting the primary job done.

A proactive employee, whether they are new to the company or have been there for years, is someone who anticipates a problem or challenge in advance and handles it...before it becomes an ordeal to fix.

A proactive employee is a manager's dream because it may be exhausting to have to think up and hand out tasks all the time. It's awesome when someone comes up with the answer and takes action before the question was even posed.

MVPs are proactive. Let's look closely at the word pro-active. In Latin, the prefix pro means forward. For example, when you make progress, you are moving forward. The second part of the word is active, meaning in motion.

MVPs actively move projects forward toward a solution. They are not held back by distractions, lack of clarity, or uncertainty of any kind. They also don't pretend to busy themselves with other things, thinking that they are being a team player when their principal task is still incomplete.

MVPs are proactive in that they do things in advance, or forward, of being told. They anticipate a problem and solve it before anybody else around them even realizes that there's a problem to be solved.

It doesn't mean that they're frantically trying to get things done all the time, it means that they're moving forward toward something that matters. MVPs consistently move forward in advance of others. They move toward that clear objective, toward specific goals, toward that MVP status.

But there is a barrier to being proactive. Well, there are a few barriers, actually. Distractions, a lack of clarity, and an uncertain future are among the biggest barriers to being proactive and the reason why people who desire to perform under-deliver.

People mean well when they tell you to be more proactive, but be warned, you will need to shift your mindset around the myth that being proactive is always the thing to do. Being proactive only counts once the original job is done and you can't get the primary job done if you are under-delivering on your promises.

The Cost Of Under-Delivering On Promises

Promises were a lot like impressions.
The second one didn't count for much.
~ Kristin Hannah, *Distant Shores*

When facilitating a leadership breakout session at a conference, I inquired of the group, "Knowing the incredible outcomes of managing a team of MVPs and how that would make you feel, what could keep you from playing consistently at the MVP level yourself?"

Crickets.

The participants thought that we were there to talk about the performance of everyone else. They themselves were in the clear, until that question hung in the air. The silence seemed to last a little too long from my perspective, but it was necessary for these individuals to consider the question and not to have people talking over their processing.

When the attendees hollered out their answers, most of them were no surprise to me, after having led so many of these conversations with different size groups across different industries.

Ironically, a gentleman who was checking his phone and not even looking up, yelled, "Distractions!"

Ah, yes, distractions are one of the three obstacles to delivering on promises that MVPs must overcome. The other two are lack of clarity and uncertainty about the future. Now clear your desk, delete all of those e-mails calling your name from that cluttered inbox, and let's first consider distractions.

Remember that being more proactive may work for you, if you direct your effort toward your fundamental role, or against you, if you are proactively doing what nobody really values in the first place.

Since you've read this far, I'm going to address you as a person who strives to be proactive in a good way, toward your main objectives. Therefore, it's important that you are familiar with the barriers that will get in your way. If you are proactively engaged in doing things that are pointless, then get ready for a wake-up call. You are about to discover why you will never reach MVP status.

Distractions

Funny thing about writing a chapter about distractions. There certainly were plenty of them that attempted to divert my attention away from writing!

On a recent coaching call, Diane, who was concerned about making her monthly quota, told me that what was getting in her way was a lack of a clear, focused goal. When I probed further, she talked about how she gets a lot of e-mails, how her phone wasn't working, and how she had to take time off of work to get the phone fixed.

I didn't hear lack of a focused goal, I heard distractions.

There are an endless number of reasons why we get distracted and an equally long list of things we do that are nothing more than distractions. Is there a simple reason why we allow distractions?

Perhaps we let distractions get the better of us because we don't believe that it is possible to achieve more. A subconscious level of doubt keeps us playing a deficient game. We doubt our abilities, so we get to justify our limited results because there is tacit agreement in the world that we could have done more, if only we were not so distracted.

It's easier to blame a lack of accomplishment on an overflowing inbox than it is to accept responsibility for not taking the actions that would have gotten you to your goal.

In some people, getting sucked into the endless vortex of distractions could present like a case of laziness, but look beyond that. Self-worth is critical to success in any endeavor. Being worthy of more, really feeling like you have what it takes to reach the intended goal, makes it a little tougher to get distracted.

Frankly, when Diane said that she didn't have a clear, discernible goal, it was a cop out. Two weeks prior to this call, she and I had discussed how her current business and the new business that she was helping her husband get off the ground could be completely altered inside of ninety days if she would make three calls per day. She was excited and pledged to make those three calls.

It turns out that she made the three calls on the day that we spoke, but she had not made a single call since. No action. No MVP trophy.

Distractions cost you. In Diane's case she estimated that she easily wasted three hours a day on distractions.

"I am hereby granting you a twenty-seven-hour day when the rest of the world only has twenty-four. What will you do with your extra three hours a day?"

Assuming that you take a swig of truth serum before answering so that you don't say something laughable like make more calls, you'd likely answer as Diane did. "I would spend more time with my kids, and my business would achieve its target sales goals so I wouldn't have to worry about money anymore."

Hmmm...

So, does Diane suffer from a lack of clarity surrounding her goal or an overabundance of distractions? It seems to me that her objective was quite unequivocal.

The things that keep us from working on our dreams are the little distractions that seem so significant at the time. Tim Ferriss, in his best-selling book *The 4-Hour Workweek*, advised people to be more in control of the time that they waste checking their e-mail. By setting up an auto-responder, letting people know that you check your e-mail at certain specific times and then following through in that way, you are more in control of the distractions that you allow in your day. This is a tip that really cuts back on the distractions.

E-mails have gotten out of hand. If you are like me, after a rejuvenating vacation you have accumulated hundreds or thousands of e-mails. Even the auto-responder announcement that you are out of the office didn't help because people wanted to get something off of their desk and on to yours.

A few years ago I decided (or re-decided) how life would work for me after a relaxing vacation. I set up a new message on my e-mail auto-responder that read, *I am going on a real vacation, which means that I won't be checking voicemail or e-mail. When I return to the office, the first thing that I'm going to do is delete all of my e-mails. If you want me to see what you just sent to me, please send it again on (date), the day after I return to work.*

The first time I experimented with this approach, I did review the e-mails to ensure that I hadn't missed a good invitation to speak at a conference or some other tremendous opportunity, but once I saw that people did honor my request and re-sent their e-mails, I have never looked back.

I love this strategy because I am able to enjoy a vacation until the end of it without having to check my e-mail every day or agonize about the pile of work that I'm coming back to upon my return.

I actually made a video of me deleting all of my e-mails with one keystroke! How liberating! Join the take back the *vacation* movement, and try it yourself!

(https://www.youtube.com/c/meritgest)

Some people objected to my vacation protection strategy, but most applauded it. Before you resist it, see if there is a new possibility available to you by re-deciding how you do vacations. I challenge you to try it!

Human beings are hard-wired to protect themselves, whether this means running from the tiger or camping out in a comfort zone. It's not that unusual for us to say that we could have been great, if only we had had the time to invest in planting the seeds of our brilliance. Of course, all of the steps between where you start and the realization of a goal may feel overwhelming.

The antidote for overwhelming is taking modest, consistent actions every single day. It really is that elementary.

Distractions rob you of achieving your full potential. You want to be the MVP of your company, but if you are under-delivering on your promises and intentions, it won't happen. Under-delivery is not a promotable attribute. People who under-deliver are stuck. They are passed over for new opportunities, challenges, and possibilities.

Distractions entice you because they keep you from dealing with areas where you are not certain of your level of competence. If you are not sure that you are good at something or will be able to find the right answer, you may procrastinate. It appears as if distractions are getting the best of you, but upon closer inspection, it's about not feeling comfortable with that kind of task.

That scenario came up a lot when I trained sales managers. Managers across countless industries complained about their sales-people not having the time to make new business development calls. They told me that their reps were bogged down with paperwork or follow-up calls, and that's why there was never any time for new business calls.

The truth is that whatever you don't have time to do is something that you are not sure you do well. These managers didn't need to give their reps less paperwork or more productivity training, they needed to work with their reps on how to make effective new business calls and practice at this with role playing.

When you are good at something, and confident in your skills, it's remarkable how much time there is to do that something. Take note of what people are being *distracted from*, and help them feel confident in that area.

Jennifer is a branch manager for a busy bank and huddles with her team daily because there are a lot of different objectives and goals to be met. She wants her team to be relaxed, feel appreciated, and accomplish their aggressive goals.

When they get together for their daily huddle, Jennifer addresses each person on her team. "Okay, what's your number one objective today? What are you going to do to move toward this objective?"

This gets everyone aligned with how to think at MVP level and how to direct their thinking toward a specific goal.

Sometimes Jennifer calls an additional huddle in the middle of the day if she feels like people have succumbed to distractions. Doing this gets everyone back to the place where they are less likely to under-deliver on promises.

The problem is not necessarily that under-deliverers don't want to or know how to over-deliver and exceed expectations, it's that they allow themselves to be so bogged down with distractions that seem important (or make them feel important) that they never get around to what would actually make them indispensable, most vital, to their organization.

Could you imagine someone saying, *I can't save the child from the burning building right now because I've got to clear seventy-six e-mails from my inbox.*

Crazy, right?

How about this one? *I'll work on that presentation that I'm delivering in front of the entire senior executive team that could catapult my career into the stratosphere as soon as I clean off my desk.*

Equally nuts.

Get a box. Dump everything on your desk into that box. Bam! You've done it. Your desk is clear. Now get to work on the presentation!

Here's how to know whether something is essential or is a distraction. Ready? Get out your highlighter, this could change the game. *If it is not directly related to one of your top five priorities, it's a distraction.*

There is no amount of time that I could spend on e-mails or organizing my office that would ever get me to my revenue goal for my business or my lofty aims of making a difference for people. I will not be known as a good friend, mother, or business expert by having a clean office or an empty inbox. I will not have better health, wealth, or relationships by having a clean office or an empty inbox.

Answering the e-mails and organizing my office may be fundamental to constructing an environment that is conducive to achieving my goals, but if I'm cleaning out my inbox or rummaging through my desk drawers instead of taking action in a direct way toward my goals, they are distractions.

Having said that, clutter was a major distraction for me on so many levels: spiritual, physical, and mental. I didn't have the patience, the time, or the inclination to take care of the clutter myself, and too much of my energy was being zapped by all of the clutter, so I re-decided how I would deal with it.

Several years ago I worked with a company called Major Organizers (you might have even seen my friend, Angela Cody-Rouget, founder of the company, on *Shark Tank!*). I hired the company to get my office organized once and for all. Best. Money. Ever. Spent.

All of my distractions were eliminated. The representative of the company put systems in place to keep everything running like clockwork. Now all I need is a semi-annual tune-up, and I'm back on track. My kitchen pantry, my garage, my basement, and even my e-mail inbox and digital filing system were all organized for me.

I'm so sorry, I didn't mean to distract you from our topic at hand, but if you are not naturally wired for organization, hire someone who is, and stop making excuses about why you are not playing the game of business or life at the level you could be.

Back to primary goals...

If I was writing a book about underwater basket weaving, and teaching others how to weave baskets underwater was not my primary goal, then writing that book would be a distraction. If I was writing a book on...well, *this* book, that counts as a primary activity that is directly linked to accomplishing my business goals. Understand the difference?

What happens when your business goals are vague? Distractions actually make us feel like we've accomplished something, but sadly, spending time on distractions rarely leads to an MVP award or feeling like an MVP.

Reading this book, by the way, is not a distraction, it's a laudable choice!

Distractions are not the only thing that keeps a person from achieving MVP status. Business people may suffer from a lack of clarity about what they want to accomplish.

Lack of Clarity

Imagine a race where the finish line is wide and fuzzy and the rules of winning are unclear. Does the runner have to cross the entire line or just touch the line? Is the runner allowed to step out of bounds and come back in? You could undoubtedly lose the race due to a technicality, even if you are Usain Bolt. Nothing hurts a competitive person more than seeing another individual get the first place trophy when that individual did not run the fastest race.

When it comes to being considered an MVP, a lack of clarity is one of the top three barriers because it is difficult to be in action toward a nebulous objective.

We all want to be certain that if we do specific things to reach our goals, they will work out well in the end. Goal-setting was always the most popular class on my training calendar because people want to be *certain* that they have chosen the right path to get them to the right goal.

The problem with certainty is that it's a backwards vantage point. We check our rearview mirror to make sure that we thought of everything and that all of our ducks are in a row. (Are ducks ever in a row? Where does that expression come from? See how easily I can be distracted!) When you do that, you don't see what's right in front of you. Certainty is a backwards facing view. You can't move forward with a backwards facing view without eventually bumping into something.

Clarity is a forward facing view. You may not know the exact path, but you see what's in front of you, which will give you more options for your route, that is if you are willing and able to re-decide a path that you recognize is not getting you where you want to go.

Clarity allows for trusting. Certainty implies a lack of trust. When you are clear about where you are headed and why it makes sense for you to go in that direction, you have the best chance of arriving because you trust in your unclouded vision. When you don't trust your path and are busy looking backwards to make sure that you have thought everything through, you're likely to get lost.

Certainty is overrated. Lack of certainty has kept many people from doing many things. It is the number one killer of possibility. *Of that I am certain!*

You will never be certain that it will all work out. Get over it. Stop trying to achieve certainty. It is unachievable.

Strive for clarity. Clarity unleashes your true potential and limitless possibilities.

There is freedom in clarity. For most of my life I have been a goal-setter. Others describe me as driven, accomplishes her goals, knows what she wants. You get the picture.

The funny thing is that I didn't always *get the picture.*

There is a certain kind of magic in pictures. You've heard millions of times that a picture is worth a thousand words. Does anyone else find it funny that people waste words to say that a picture is worth a thousand words instead of just drawing a picture? It wasn't until I started drawing pictures that I really understood the meaning of that cliché.

You have probably already heard that we are all either left-brained or right-brained. Well, we may lean one way or the other, but unless you've had a lobotomy or suffered such a traumatic experience in your early development years that quite literally stopped one area of your brain from its normal development, you are most likely in the vast majority of people who have a complete brain. (I can think of a few guys I dated for whom the jury is still out on the anatomy of their brains, but I digress...)

While it's generally true that we all have a complete brain, we tend to be somewhat one-sided, either overly analytical (left-brained) or highly emotional/creative (right-brained). We learn to accept how we are wired, and we tend to play to our strengths.

A left-brained person makes their way through the world by making sense of the data, analyzing the facts, and organizing the pieces of their life puzzle. A right-brained person uses creativity and imagination to plan and prepare. Left-brains make lists, right-brains make mind-map pictures.

Why have I always written goals on paper if I tend to be more right-brained? I was using a left-brained list-making strategy though I was more of an intuitive, outside-the-box thinker. The strategy was working for me, until I learned about using my whole brain to get what I want and to have more fun getting there. All I had to do was draw.

With my son's crayons and a blank sheet of paper, I thought about what I wanted in my life, and then I drew it. It's surprising what you can learn when you allow your subconscious mind to be heard. The way to listen to your subconscious mind is through the pictures on your paper.

Allow me to leave the business world for a moment to demonstrate the power of your subconscious mind and how best to communicate with it.

Dr. Bernie S. Siegel, author of *Love, Medicine & Miracles* and founder of ECaP (Exceptional Cancer Patients), studies the pictures that patients draw to understand in advance if their treatment will work. His fascinating, yet straightforward, research is eye-opening to consider.

When patients depicted their doctor as the devil or the injections as black in color, Dr. Siegel knew that they were in trouble and that it was highly unlikely that their treatment would be successful. On the other hand, when a patient drew a blue (a healthy color) X-ray machine emitting a yellow ray (a spiritual color) into her body, Dr. Siegel knew that the patient anticipated a positive result from the treatment.

So, why aren't businesspeople drawing? Heck, if Dr. Siegel's cancer patients are discovering how their subconscious mind is helping or hurting them in the treatment of a deadly disease, surely there is value for businesspeople in drawing their relationships with prospects and clients, not to mention their relationship to their company, to industry, and to money.

Since our minds think in pictures, when we decide what we want we may need a new visual depiction of the vision that we are now moving toward. This may also work in reverse. When you are unclear about what you really want, perhaps it is time to get out some markers, crayons, or paint and start dreaming on paper about where you are headed.

I know how hokey that sounds. This concept was deleted and then inserted back in several times during the writing of this book. My experience tells me that if one person might not appreciate the value of this practice, another reader might think that it is the missing piece that unlocks the possibilities that they couldn't access. So in it stays. Please feel free to skip the art activity if it doesn't resonate with you.

In Cathy and Gary Hawk's *Get Clarity for Life* and *Work Retreat*, I was among several business owners learning about the Clarity International® tools described in their book *Get Clarity*. Given only thirty minutes to draw our life's vision, it was spectacular what the individuals in our group drew.

I didn't know that I wanted to live at a spa resort where people would come from around the world for retreats, relaxation, and recreation, but there it was. It was not necessary to know how I would get there, just that I am headed there. Stay tuned...

If I re-decide along the way, so be it. For now, I'm getting a kick out of seeing it several times a day when I look at the drawing hanging in my office. I don't think that it was an accident that I was invited to present a program at the International Spa Association conference, do you?

Imagine if I wrote *live at a spa* on a goals worksheet? There would be so many steps and too much internal conversation in my own mind saying that this is not really possible, and the vision might fizzle away. Dismissed as something impossible. In fact, the idea came to me years ago, but I let it drift away because it didn't seem realistic.

Suddenly, I find myself living ninety minutes away from the Rocky Mountains of Colorado. A friend and business colleague of mine, Mike Hawkins, award-winning author of *Activating Your Ambition and the SCOPE of Leadership* book series, built a corporate retreat center called Alpine Villa Retreat in the most beautiful mountain town of Breckenridge, Colorado, where his clients may bring their leadership teams to a state-of-the-art training facility, complete with hot tub for twenty, gourmet kitchen, and massage therapists on speed dial. And yes, he lives there full time. *Hmmm...it really is possible.*

The vision never left me, I just suppressed it. But my subconscious mind has been working on it since the day I first came up with the kooky idea. I am living in Colorado and know someone who has already done a version of what I want to do. Coincidence? I think not.

What you focus on expands. The pictures you feed your mind are the to-do lists for your subconscious brain. It's not up to you to figure out how you will make the picture a reality, your only job is to paint the picture of what you want and trust that you will be led to the right actions and people to get it done.

Clarity moves you toward your vision. Clarity generates action.

Uncertainty About The Future

In many of the same ways that a lack of clarity may derail a person from being proactive as an MVP, a murky future has the same impact. The distinction between a lack of clarity and a hazy future is the level of perceived control.

You are in the driver's seat when it comes to being clear about your objectives. Even if the goals are not your own, as is the case in the overall goal of a company or a department goal, you may be in control of and responsible for the specific actions that you must take to meet that goal.

The idea of an uncertain future is distinct. It is a barrier that keeps people from being more proactive toward their primary objectives because it gets in the way of people taking action and reacting to circumstances in a resourceful way. Remember, it's not bad to be proactive, but if you think that you are being proactive when, in fact, you have not completed your number one job due to distractions, lack of clarity, or uncertainty about the future, then being proactive isn't doing you any good.

For example, Larry was uncertain about his future with the company he worked for due to its recent acquisition by a larger competitor. He felt helpless and vulnerable regarding his future. Feeling helpless is not a precursor to being proactive in a positive way, it actually has the opposite effect. Job insecurity leads to frustration, burnout, and limited feelings of engagement at work.

Larry's manager, Arlene, picked up on his lack of participation and questioned his loyalty. Fortunately, they talked about the situation, and Arlene was able to ease Larry's fears about job security which, once relieved, allowed him to be more proactive (again, doing his most important tasks first) at work without the concern of losing his job.

Managers, take note, the more your team feels that job security might be an issue, the less likely they will be able to focus on their primary job much less be a proactive problem solver.

Under-delivering on promises is not a promotable attribute. To avoid this eliminate all distractions, gain clarity about your primary objectives, and don't wait to be certain to be in action.

SHIFT
STARTERS

- Articulate your top three to five goals in order to identify what is a distraction and what is in alignment with your goals.

- Minimize the distractions from your business day and work space.

- Get clarification about any current vague business objectives.

- Get clear about your primary job. What is it *really* that you get a paycheck for doing?

- Construct a vision for your personal future with the company. You get extra credit for drawing a picture of your vision.

- Remember, extra credit only counts when your original job is complete. Look for places where you put off doing what needs to be done in favor of a distraction or being proactive in another area at the expense of your primary role.

Bonus Business Leader Shifts:

- Do you need a culture shift? Make sure that you create a culture that acknowledges when people are proactive toward their main objectives and highlights that they went above and beyond only after their primary job was done.

- Shift the thinking around what are distracting activities versus MVP activities, and share the difference between the two with your staff.

- Provide clarity to your employees about your business objectives. You may have to shift your thinking in terms of rewarding and acknowledging people for doing the right kind of proactive work at the right time.

- Remove any uncertainty regarding job security for your team to the extent that you are able.

4

Meeting Standards Doesn't Cut It Anymore

...the best is a matter of standards—and I set my own standards.
~ Ayn Rand, *The Fountainhead*

Every month when I pay my mortgage I am reminded that meeting the standards is the minimum level of what is acceptable. It is a subtle but constant reminder that making the monthly payment is fine, but *would you like to make an additional payment toward your principle?* stares at me month after month, taunting me. Meeting the standard of making my mortgage payment on time isn't an achievement, it's a responsibility. It's what needs to be done.

Meeting my standards for going out to dinner on my anniversary, my birthday, and Valentine's Day isn't going to get my husband into the Hubby Hall of Fame. Setting out cold cuts and a bag of chips may qualify in some worlds as a Super Bowl party, but it would only be meeting the minimum expectations of football fans.

Hitting your monthly sales quota is what is expected of you as a salesperson. It might appear that you are meeting your standard if nobody else on the team is making their numbers, but it doesn't qualify as an accomplishment worth recognizing. It's the requirement of the job. Hey, don't shoot the messenger, it's the truth. Do you want to be an undisputed MVP? Find a way to exceed your quota, in spite of whatever challenges come your way.

Here's the straight talk you need to hear… it is a myth that meeting the standards is good enough for an MVP. I have heard countless people complaining about not being rewarded for doing a good job when all they did was the standard job. Seriously. I hate to be the bad guy, but you don't set yourself apart by doing what everyone else is doing. Anyone can send a client a holiday card, but hardly anyone sends a card to mark the anniversary of the day they started doing business together.

In an *everyone gets a trophy for participating* world, you want to lead a team, or be the person on the team who *earns* the MVP trophy. Meeting standards is the ticket to entry, it's not a cause for reward.

Don't get me wrong, I'm not suggesting that you can't or shouldn't celebrate accomplishing a goal, but meeting the expected level of production is not representative of MVP-level performance.

There is only one MVP on the winning Super Bowl team. It took everyone on the team to win the game, but only one player gets the Most Valuable Player award. That player didn't meet expectations on the field that day, he exceeded expectations. It's the same thing in your organization.

Find out what it looks and feels like to meet the standards in your role in your company. Find out what it looks and feels like to under-perform (through stories, not personal experience!).

Sure, a C is a passing grade, but I believe that most parents would tell you that the C represents the minimal standard of what is acceptable. You may make the minimum payment on your credit card bill every month, but it will take you a long time to pay off the bill, and any cost savings that you might have realized by buying in bulk are lost to finance charges.

But wait a minute. What's wrong with meeting standards and being satisfied with doing the required job and calling it great? Nothing at all is wrong with that, except if you want more possibilities for personal and professional growth. In that case, being satisfied with meeting standards will sabotage your future possibilities. Meeting standards is not a promotable quality in today's competitive marketplace.

My editor thought that I should add more to this chapter, but I thought that it was more in keeping with the theme if I just wrote the minimum acceptable amount. Ah, author humor...

SHIFT
STARTERS

- Shift your expectations: What are the minimal acceptable levels of activities and results in your current role? What are your expectations of yourself as an MVP?

- Do you know what your customers and clients expect of you personally and of your company? Do they need a shift in thinking about what you can actually deliver or do you need to modify your actions to match their expectations?

- Identify what other people have done to exceed expectations. Where can you make a shift to match them?

Satisfaction: Is It
The Silent Killer Of Success?

You can't have everything. Where would you put it?
~ Steven Wright

Always, the moment that I heard the Rolling Stones sing *You can't always get what you want*, I immediately turned the radio dial to another station. It always bothered me that the Rolling Stones were mega-famous rock stars singing to us little people about how we can't always get what we want while they were likely living their colossal dreams in a princely way.

As you grow older, you realize that the truth is, *you can't want everything there is to have.* This gives you a new perspective, and you start getting clear about what you really do want. That clarity pushes you to find ways of thinking about things and about what you are doing to get what you've always wanted.

When you are surrounded by people who think that meeting standards and staying the course are good enough, it's harder to stop and think about what might be possible beyond what you are doing now.

If the people around you are satisfied with their business and personal life, good for them. If you want more, then see them less. They won't push you toward more because it will make them feel like they are doing less.

Before finishing this manuscript I started spending more time with my author friends, and being the only unpublished one in the bunch was no longer acceptable...for any of us! MVPs want to be around other MVPs.

I interrupt this book about shifting your thinking about common business myths to bring you front-page information that is absolutely not a myth, in my opinion and as I have found in my research. You are heavily influenced by the books you read and the company you keep. Choose your influencers wisely. People around you may be satisfied because they have to be. They are stuck. You may need to re-visit your relationships and find people who are satisfied and yet are still striving for more.

As I've mentioned before, my job as a trainer, coach, consultant, and speaker has always been first and foremost to be the Chief Belief Officer, the person who believes that more is possible for the people I work with. In time, my clients begin to see what I see for them, and that's when the techniques that I've taught them start to stick.

Most people who have willingly enrolled themselves in sessions with me over the years honestly wanted to improve their skills, make more money, and do so with less effort and more fun.

Early in my career I was introduced to Pamela, a wealthy woman who lived in Chicago's affluent North Shore community. Her husband made plenty of money, and she was a successful recruiter in her own right. She had boatloads of stuff. She went on luxurious vacations. Money was not an issue in her household, so it struck me as funny when she wanted me to coach her to be a more effective salesperson and transform her from achieving moderate results to MVP status.

She convinced me that she was committed, and we set up a coaching plan. She showed up to the first session, but that was it. I was confused because she paid in full up front, so my expectation was that she would want to take advantage of what she had paid for. I chased her for a while and heard...nothing. Silence.

The only explanation that I could come up with was that she was satisfied with her current situation and that it wasn't worth the effort to her to do, be, or have anything more.

You can't always get what you (say) you want.

Maybe what you think you want isn't what would really make you happy. For Pamela, it was stylish to have a business coach and build an identity in the marketplace confirming *I'm a player*, but satisfaction will kill you when it comes to taking action.

It is possible to be satisfied with today and still strive for more tomorrow. In Pamela's case, she was satisfied with today and satisfied if tomorrow looked the same. For her, satisfaction was the silent killer of success.

In the case of another client, Jim, he was satisfied with the performance of his sales team during a trade show, but he knew that his team could build on their current results with some trade show training. Even though he was satisfied today, he recognized that he would not be satisfied with the same results tomorrow, so he took action, and we got to work making the team working the trade show better prepared for success.

Satisfaction can kill, but it can also catapult you into immediate action. It all depends on how you see the situation today from the perspective of tomorrow. (More on that in Part III.)

Are you satisfied with this chapter, or are you left wanting more?

I love when people are satisfied and happy but still on the hunt for more. It's a fine line, I know. As a business owner, some days I think that I want to have massive influence, an over-packed speaking schedule of international engagements, and a TV show (who doesn't want to be on TV?). On other days a lifestyle business without all the hustle and bustle would be fine with me.

Then I consider today's action plan from the perspective of the results that I want tomorrow, and I get back to work. Can you relate?

SHIFT
STARTERS

- Ask three different people with whom you interact in business if they are satisfied with your product or service or is there some shift you could make that would be better.

- Notice their level of enthusiasm with being satisfied.
  Has anything shifted by you asking the question?
  Has anything shifted by you taking new or different action?

- Are they satisfied enough to do more business with you?

- Do you feel a shift inside yourself when you are satisfied versus thrilled?

Winners Do The Extra Credit, Even When They Have Already Earned An A

You can't control your level of talent,
but you can control your level of effort.
~ Thomas Blake, father of James Blake, tennis pro

Hey, since it's the chapter on Extra Credit,
I added an extra quote!

There are no traffic jams along the extra mile.
~ Roger Staubach

More than twenty-five years ago, Robert Fulghum published a credo that became a #1 New York Times bestseller that sold more than seven million copies world-wide. The book is called *All I Really Need to Know I Learned in Kindergarten.* I was a bit of a late bloomer, so we're going to talk about what I learned in middle school.

Well, technically, it was my son's middle school, so I wasn't kidding about being a late bloomer.

My son Jake is a bright boy who has always done just enough to get by. Like most of his friends, he is always in a hurry to finish his homework and go out to play. As we looked at his grades one day, which overall were good, I noted that he was doing poorly in science.

But he assured me that I shouldn't worry because he could always do the extra credit. At the same time he was getting an A in math, so he told me that there was no need to do the extra credit in that subject.

I thought about all of the salespeople, sales managers, business owners, and executives I've coached over the years, all of the high-achievers in the public eye, all of the scientists, inventors, entrepreneurs who have done miraculous things, and I told Jake that *winners do the extra credit, even when they have already earned an A.*

Sure, you may graduate with a B or a C. Sure, you may renew a contract doing only what you promised. Sure, you may provide the expected level of service and value, but you'll never really know what you're made of, you'll never really impact the people around you and raise them up, you'll never really know what could have been possible if you had done the extra credit. More is possible.

In 1998 I joined a sales and sales management training business. Day in and day out I taught companies how to hire salespeople, develop sales processes, and manage sales teams. Everyone learned the same strategies. Everyone used the same behavior metrics. Everyone had access to the same coaching support. And that's when the secret to consistent sales success was revealed.

It wasn't the technique, though it was needed. It wasn't the behaviors, though they helped. It wasn't the products or services, though they were necessary. It wasn't the economy or the marketplace, though that factored in. It was what we all learned in middle school. *Do the extra credit, even when you have already earned an A.*

Doing extra credit is not about doing more stuff all at the same time or being a multi-tasker. There are people out there who do a whole lot of nothing. I call them multi-slackers! Multi-slackers may lounge on the couch, do nothing, and avoid responsibility...*all at the same time.* It's astonishing!

Multi-slackers in the office are a unique breed. They think that they are getting a lot done...

"I was at work, multi-slacking, when my boss walked over to me, and I had to shove a bunch of stuff off of my desk and look busy doing something in less than five seconds. Whew! What a rush!"

And, of course, his multi-slacking friend has a splendid comeback. "Wow! You have to teach me how to do that, except that I'm busy not doing much, waiting for something else to not do, and thinking a little about all the things that I'm not going to do. But now is not a good time...because I'm too busy doing nothing."

Do you know people like this too?

The MVPs of the company handle projects beyond their current experience level. They are not necessarily given the projects, they go out and get them. They don't wait for opportunities, they create them.

Best advice ever: help your manager do what her manager requires her to get done. This is probably something that a manager once told me.

According to an article in *Psychology Today*, high-achievers are marked by a strong motive to achieve, and less accomplished individuals are often more motivated to avoid failure. Think about that for a moment. People who accomplish more are not overly concerned about failing, they are busy moving forward. People who produce less pour so much of their energy into avoiding failure that there is precious little left to propel them to success.

Remember filling out your college applications? Colleges wanted to know about your extra-curricular activities. Oh, you were an Eagle Scout, that took extra effort. Oh, you were the captain of the debate team and the star running back on the football team, plus an A student. That took something extra. Oh, you were just an A student, that's nice. Next.

Top universities look for students who do more than excel in academics. They know that having an attitude of doing extra credit even when you have already earned an A is something that will follow a student through their career and their life. It's an attitude that generates action. These kids know that to get good grades plus accomplish all of the extras, you don't waste time trying to avoid failure, you get busy moving toward your goal.

Twenty-three years ago, while backpacking around the world, I found myself in Penang, Malaysia, for a Hindu festival called Thaipusam. I had never heard of that yearly event before, and it's not likely that I'll ever forget it now.

Thaipusam is about faith, endurance, and penance. Hindus of all castes and cultures perform masochistic rituals to show their appreciation to one of their Gods, Lord Murugan, a son of Shiva. In exchange for Lord Murugan answering their prayers, many followers carry *paal kudam*, which are little pots of milk, through the streets of the city. *I know, it's not how I typically say thank you, either.*

Now, that doesn't sound so bad, except that what I didn't tell you was that these devotees carried these pots of milk on hooks...that were laced through their flesh. Called *kavadi bearers*, these men pierced their tongues and cheeks with sharp metal spikes. They hung the pots of milk on the hooks sunk into their chests and hooks in their backs, which were then attached to ropes that went around the waist of another man walking behind...and *leaning back.*

In a Malaysian newspaper I read a story about a man who vowed to carry the kavadi for as long as he lived if his daughter could have children. Apparently it worked, because the woman had eleven kids! (A mere eight kids away from having her own TV show!)

Don't get nervous, I'm not advocating that we all carry pots of milk on hooks fastened to our flesh down the office corridors. (Of course, if you try it, please send a photo!)

What I am advocating is that we understand why going the extra mile to demonstrate appreciation is important, acknowledge the role it plays in growing business, and figure out strategies to put appreciation back in our everyday conversations at work and at home.

Extra credit may be a team effort too. How's this for a slogan? *Extra credit, it's not just for individuals anymore.* Please feel free to tweet this ingenious new slogan!

People who exceed expectations give more because it's who they are, not because they are keeping score. It's an expression of who they are.

It used to be that when you were a good performer you got good rewards. Poor performers got poor rewards. The world has changed. Sometimes good performers get poor rewards and poor performers get good rewards, but what hasn't changed is that outstanding performers almost always get outstanding rewards. People who are vital to a business are acknowledged accordingly.

The gap from poor performer to good performer is considerable. A person would need to develop a lot of skills to go from being a poor performer to being a good performer. Going from good to excellent is also a giant leap, but going from excellent to outstanding is a *decision*.

If you know deep inside that you have more potential than what you are currently demonstrating, re-decide how you wish to be defined, and then do the work to move to the next level up.

But what if there is nowhere to go? No way to move up the ladder? No promotion? Do it anyway. You must demonstrate outstanding performance first. Some people have to perform for at least two years at the level at which they would like to be promoted to in order to get to that level.

Dress and train for your next job. Do the work. Have the mindset of a manager before being offered the job as manager. Have the mindset of a CEO before becoming a CEO. Have the mindset of where you want to go *before* you get there.

That is how it's done. Any confident, outstanding achiever who is in the role that you want to be in will tell you the same. They did the job that they wanted before they officially got the title.

Here's where the shift in your thinking comes in. *Act as if* may work for you, but it may not fool your inner voice because your inner voice knows that you are acting. Instead of acting as if you already have the job or client, *anticipate as if* you did. Anticipate the needs, issues, and solutions. Solve the problems in advance, as if you already had the job or the client.

The MVP of a team or a company doesn't only consider *what else may I do?* They anticipate what needs to be done, and they take care of it.

MVP Of Effort Scorecard

When managers use the MVP Of Effort Scorecard with their teams, there is often a discrepancy between what the manager thinks and what the employee thinks in terms of the level of effort that the employee gives to the job.

If your organization is like most groups I speak to, we could divide any given team into thirds. One third of the team is fully engaged. These people are with you no matter what, they're tracking with you 100 percent. They love what they're doing, they get up in the morning, they're enthusiastic, they get to work, and the excitement bubbles over. You've got those people, right? You might even be one of them!

The next third is somewhat engaged. You make a request of these folks to do something, they'll get it done. They sometimes have a good day and sometimes not so good a day. Sometimes they're delighted, and sometimes they're not.

And then there's the third that isn't engaged, and it's like pulling teeth to get these members of the team to do something, anything, even the things that are completely within their job description.

According to the Society for Human Resource Management, a fully engaged employee is going to give you 20 percent more productivity than a somewhat engaged employee.

Let's explore what an A player does compared to an F player, and while we are at it, let's shine some light on the levels in between.

An F player constantly complains about his job. Consider the job of the donut maker. His job is to open the store and make the donuts. His nametag says Donut Maker, it was the job for which he interviewed, but all he does is complain. *Can you believe that I have to make donuts? All day long?* Uh, yeah, it's on your nametag, that's what you do, that's your job. And yet, day after day, all he does is complain about making donuts. This guy is an F player. Have you ever met one of these people?

But wait, there's something even worse than an F player. Brace yourself. What's worse than an F player is a G player. Guess what G stands for? Gone. Gone, they should be gone, and here's why. They not only complain, they whine, *That's not my job.* The F player complains about his job, but at least he is doing it. But the G player won't do the job...or any job...even if it really is his actual job. See the difference?

I have never seen or heard of any circumstance where a G player ever made it much closer to the front of the alphabet. A person inclined to whine *it's not my job* is not hard-wired to think *what else may I do? in his job.* No matter what the job is, don't be fooled. Get rid of him.

It's not likely that a G player would have read this book this far, but if you feel like a G player in your current role, you aren't doing anyone any favors by staying there.

What do you think a D player might reply if you request that she do something? A D player would state *I'll do it, but I really don't want to.* She will do what you told her to do, but she will do it with a bit of resentment. It's like when my 13-year-old gives me the eye-roll any time I ask him to do something that takes him away from video games or friends.

When you get the eye-roll, the D player is thinking, *I'll do it, but I'm not going to like it, and I'm not going to like you, and I'm not going to like my customers today, and no one's going to get a good attitude out of me because I don't want to do this task, and I'm going to let you know that.*

That's a D player. No passive-aggressive D player known to man has ever gone on to become an MVP in that same role. She may have MVP qualities lurking within her, but she is saving them for another job. You won't see them in her current role.

How would you describe a C player? He is the sneaky one because what you get when you ask him to do something is...just what you asked for. No more. No less. What's wrong with someone doing what I wanted him to do, you might question? Nothing, except that you begin to think that that's all there is. You lose sight of what else might be possible. You settle for employees and purchase orders and customers that are okay but not phenomenal. You settle into the idea of *this is as good as it gets* when it is average at best.

Many times companies invite me in because they've got a whole team of C players, and they have been fine with that, until now. In some cases, they have come to believe that C players are the best that's out there, and they've lost sight of the fact that a C is average, and you don't always have to settle for average.

One CEO recently told me, "I'm fine with people who come in and just get their job done."

Some companies invite me in so that I may teach their managers how to deal more effectively with the C players on their teams. Well, for starters, see the C players for what they are. It's sensational that they get the job done, but what would happen if you granted them the space to do a little extra? What could be possible then? What if you conditioned your C players so that they were clear about what the B players and D players are doing and how they could put themselves on their own trajectory toward excellence?

So much more is possible. Most people want to feel the success that comes with giving more, being more, and achieving more. For some people it really doesn't feel good at the end of the day to come in and do what's required, nothing more, nothing less. This may leave people feeling empty, like they have more to offer but no outlet for it.

C players may only do what is expected of them because the culture of the organization is not supportive of extra-credit effort. For example, Billy was a new customer service rep in a busy retail store. After he was done going above and beyond to serve a customer, his manager took him aside and reprimanded him for spending too much time with one customer.

This sent a confusing message to Billy, especially since the store was not busy that day. Shouldn't he do whatever it takes to deliver quality customer service? Or should he spend only three minutes with a customer? Billy's manager took a potential A+ player and attempted to turn him into a solid C player. This could have conceivably derailed Billy's entire career plan!

Better than a C player would, of course, be a B player. A B player is going to do what is expected, and she is going to do it with some enthusiasm.

When I invite large audiences or smaller management teams to consider what grade they would give to people who do what is required of them with enthusiasm, they typically think that I am talking about an A player. What could be better than someone doing what is expected of them willingly? Doesn't that sounds like an A player to you?

If a B player is someone who does what is required of her, and does it enthusiastically with a good attitude, then what is an A player?

An A player would tender the question, *Is there anything else that I may do for you?* An A player is going to interject all the time, *What else may I do? What else may I learn? I want to do something more. I already finished that.* Now do you see the difference between C, B, and A players?

It's easy to pin the responsibility on the employee to bring extra-credit effort, but she will only do this as long as she is working for a manager and working in an environment that is conducive to grooming and nurturing MVPs. It may be either the employee that needs the adjustment or the environment.

I had a woman supervisor a long time ago, and her employees were always on top of it. *What may I do? How may I do more? What more may I learn?* She invariably answered us with some version of *Just shut up and do your job.* Not a pleasant way to go through life!

None of her employees stayed for very long, and every one of them talked about her behind her back! Not only was she not an MVP leader, she took an MVP team and turned it into a team of C players! Not to mention that she made her own job twice as hard, since she had rendered her department a revolving door and constantly had to replace people as they departed, thinking to herself...*good riddance.*

In my early career as a manager, I remember feeling a little pressure at times when A players continually pestered me about what else could be done. Though I knew better than to tell them to shut up and do your job, I still felt the stress of figuring it out for them. That's when another manager colleague helped me discover the difference between an A player and an A+ player.

An A player queries, *What else may I do?* An A+ player just gets it done. A+ players anticipate what you need, what the customers need, what the community needs, what their co-workers need, and they get it done.

A+ players do not run to their manager or boss to find out what needs to be done, they put themselves in the position to notice what needs to be done, and they make it happen.

It's the store clerk who grabs the broom, noticing that the floor needs to be swept. It's the teacher who attends his students' baseball games on the weekend because it will mean something to the child's sense of belonging. It's the volunteer who helps at the bake sale and improves the set-up, which moves more cookies.

When a problem arises, what does an A, B, or C player do? Any of them might head to the manager's office as their first line of defense.

What does an A+ player think? *The manager doesn't need to be bothered about it, because I'll have handled it already.*

Now, here's the problem. Have you ever been in a situation where you handled something, and it didn't turn out the way that you intended? It can backfire, right?

Imagine how you would feel if you did something above and beyond what was required of you and you got reprimanded? Not likely that you would look for anything extra ever again. This should be remembered because, as a manager, you may have to gently correct an action that was performed with good intentions but that was not what you wanted.

Sharon is a personal banker with a major bank. The number one objective for the branch is to offer superior customer service, in addition to meeting all other sales goals.

Sharon thinks out loud. "We want exceptional customer service ratings. What else could I do to make that happen? I feel like my desk is really far away from where the customers walk into the branch. That is probably not the best way to make a good first impression. What if I move my desk so that I'm next to the door? That way when the customer comes in, I'm right there with a smile on my face, and they have a better experience from the get-go."

Sharon moved her desk to the front of the branch, giving her manager two choices. The manager could yell at her, *Who told you that you could move your desk? Go back to where you were. That's not how we do things here.* and completely crush any A+ spirit lurking around. Or, as was the case in this scenario, the manager could choose to be responsible for the communication and deliberately endorse an environment where it was possible for somebody to show up ready, willing, and able to bring that MVP level of performance.

Sharon moved her desk, and the impact on her customer service ratings was immediately noticeable and positive. That's an A+ player all day long. She handled a problem that nobody else even knew was a problem. Kudos to her manager, who encouraged the action, thereby creating more opportunities for the rest of the staff to bring their A+ game.

But Sharon didn't stop there, as is typical, because most A+ players don't ever stop. Sharon took it one level further. One of the standard practices that has made this particular bank so highly regarded in the industry is that employees complete a detailed profile for every customer. Some bankers are better than others at filling out the form, but Sharon loads up the profile with every detail she possibly can. Sharon dives deep, she questions the customer, and she does a magnificent job of filling out the profiles in incredible detail.

Now when she's out of the branch and someone else is filling in for her, all this person has to do is go in to a customer's records, and they are blown away by the details found in the customer profile. The customer has an experience of being known even though the banker has just met them! That's how A+ players roll.

When management at the bank thinks about somebody to whom more opportunity should be given, somebody who is on the fast-track, somebody who can grow and develop in her career, is Sharon at the top of the list? Absolutely.

Now, here's the thing, managers need to share these stories with others. Sharon had the idea to move her desk closer to the door. She saw an opportunity, and she took advantage of it. That's an MVP player, and if, as a manager, you can share these kinds of anecdotes and stories from within one department or branch or office to another, it opens the door to what other people will think of as a possibility. The way it is now, many people have to be told what to do and how to do it.

Wouldn't it be better if all of the other employees were told, "Here's the story of an MVP in our company. She saw a problem, she saw an opportunity, she acted on it, and she didn't worry about being reprimanded because our culture supports being proactive when it is directly related to doing your primary job well.

Bringing A+ effort to your job doesn't mean that you are working harder or getting more than your job done. It means that you are getting the *right* job done. It means that you are connecting your work to the most important objective and discovering what you can add to reach that objective faster, easier, or with a little more flare and fun.

Act on your ideas. If you need to tweak them later, okay, but you will be best served when you act on them today. People need to know, especially the younger generation coming into the work force for the first time, what it looks like to really bring your best self to your daily work.

It takes more than just showing up to earn the MVP.

Manager Activity

Take a look at the chart below, and spend a moment grading each member of your current team, and yourself, on the level of MVP effort that you've seen demonstrated. I specifically encourage you to examine just the level of effort that people bring to their role.

This isn't taking into consideration how well they know their job or how long they've been with you. There are many, many other facets to performance management and performance improvement. We're specifically isolating the level of effort that a person brings to his job to determine if he is an A player. Being an A+ player is just one aspect of being an MVP.

	Description
A+	Anticipates and does without being asked
A	Asks, *What else may I do?*
B	Does what is asked with enthusiasm
C	Does only what is asked, rarely more
D	Does what is asked with resentment
F	Complains while doing their job
G (Gone)	Doesn't do the job and whines, *That's not my job!*

Have people self-assess to determine if your perception matches theirs. Go through their rationale with them so that they may understand the distinctions between an A+ and a G player, and then you may have a constructive dialogue about what it means to perform at that next level up.

Okay, we've covered a lot of ground in Part II. Being more proactive only counts when your original job is done. When you are proactively solving problems in your primary role then your enemies are distractions, lack of clarity and uncertainty about the future. Being more proactive in your primary job only to meet the standards may be satisfying but it will not make you an MVP.

Yes, winners do the extra credit even when they already have earned an A, but they also know that to stay in action, they must be upbeat and more positive...or, as you are about to discover in Part III... just positive enough.

SHIFT
STARTERS

- Self-assess your level of effort according to the A+ player through G player system outlined in this chapter.

- What attitude and behavior changes do you need to make to move toward A+ player status?

- Once your primary job is done, help your manager complete some of his tasks, or help your client in some way that she is not expecting.

Be More Positive

Or Just Positive Enough

PART III

Myth #3

Be More Positive

Some people see the glass half full. Others see it half empty.
I see a glass that's twice as big as it needs to be.
~ George Carlin

Early in my career, I had a boss in the advertising business who motivated people with scare tactics. He never had a sense of optimism that the team of people whom he led could actually get the job done. He was the general manager of a major radio station in Chicago, the third largest market in the country. He was notorious for his obnoxious rants and his fiery temper.

Having been highly successful in a sales role, I found myself in the fast-lane and was offered a management position. Instead of having a buffer of two layers of management between the loathsome general manager and me, there would only be one. This was certainly an unbelievable opportunity at such an early stage in my career, but this guy spent his days screaming maniacally at people and dysfunctional processes (that he put into place).

The vibe around the office said that the team didn't have what it took to be successful, so he yelled at everyone to get us going. I always found it strange that he didn't believe in anyone, no matter what their role, when he had had the final word when it came to hiring every single person in the first place.

As it turned out, I was offered another management position with a different radio station at virtually the same time. The station was called Personal Achievement Radio, and the general manager couldn't have been more of a sweetheart to work with. He was an optimist, he believed in the people we brought on board to reach the station's aggressive goals, and he was also able to sort through the facts in a non-judgmental way.

In fact, more than twenty years later, I'm still fond of and in contact with Tony Jacobs, the world's best boss ever. We had fun, we made money, and I learned more about managing and getting results from people than I ever would have under the management style of the raving lunatic.

There is more to the conversation of being nice or nasty than just optimism versus pessimism or seeing the glass half-full or half-empty. It doesn't matter how much liquid is in the glass, what matters is what *kind* of liquid is in the glass! Oh, sorry, that was off topic. What I meant to say is that it's what you make *half-full* or *half-empty* mean in your life.

I suppose that I could have worked for the deranged tormentor and tried to stay positive, *but why?* He was in the business of breaking people down, and I've always been in the business of building people up. I'm typically a glass half-full kind of gal, but it's what I've made that mean that matters.

As a young person just starting out, I was unwilling to let anyone rain on my parade. The reason why the bully offered me the promotion was the very reason why I couldn't accept the job. I have a natural ability to see possibilities, and that's what he wanted at the management level. It was the thing that I wasn't willing to risk losing working under his leadership.

Have you ever seen a mature person completely devoid of the ability to consider new possibilities and options? I have. It's not pretty. It's pretty sad and, though I was young and hungry for opportunities,

I could see the reality of what working in that environment would do to my spirit. I'm grateful that I had the courage to turn the job down.

The glass is half-full could mean, *Perfect, I have room for more fabulous stuff to fill the glass!* Or it could just as easily mean, *Oh sure, it's half-full, but I'll still have to bust my butt to keep filling it up.* In the second scenario, you still see that the glass is half-full, but you also see the work required to keep it that way.

An overly optimistic person (I like to call them Pollyanna, but more about that later) sees the good everywhere, no matter how much or how little is in the glass. *Oh, goodie, there is just a drop in this glass! What fantastic news! Oh, joy, this glass is overflowing! What incredible news!* Viewing life through an optimistic lens means that no matter what life throws at you, you will see the good that will come of the situation because you are willing to search for it.

A realistic person doesn't notice the good in the situation because she sees the probable setbacks and all of the work that will be necessary along the way. *Who cares how much is in the glass? It's going to take a lot of work to fill it up.*

The third myth that MVPs have learned to shift their thinking around is to *be more positive.* You must be willing to be a card-carrying optimist, but too much of that good thing isn't a good thing. You will not see possibilities if your frame of mind is overly realistic and focuses only on the work required. The key is to be just the right amount of both optimistic and realistic.

If it appears that the optimists you know make more money and have more fun, there is a reason for this. They see things working out in advance of the result, and that motivates them to keep going, take action, and move forward. With their momentum, they eventually succeed.

They manifest more possibilities because they believed that it could work out. With that belief, they took action. With that action, they produced results. With those results, they believed that they could do more, so they took more action, and that shifted their thinking about what was possible, and they kept going. The cycle continues.

When you view the world through an overly realistic lens the same cycle works, but it works against you. One bad thing happens, you dwell on it, then another bad thing happens, and you get more evidence that bad things keep happening to you. Now two negative things have happened to you, and rather than thinking about them as separate and unrelated occurrences, you have evidence to justify how bad things always happens to you.

Always and *Never* are dangerous words.

For example, you *always* miss the bus. Your boss *always* wants more details. You *always* spill your coffee. Really? Always? Or was there one time, just one time, when that wasn't true? If you can come up with one example of a time when you enjoyed a cup of coffee without spilling it, then you can't say that you *always* spill it.

If you can chip away at a negative pattern, sooner or later you can make a dent in it, and then you can pulverize it completely and eventually turn it into just the right amount of both optimistic and realistic.

Your new belief could be *I drink my coffee most of the time without spilling it*. After a while, the old belief that you always spill your coffee will disappear.

Detroit has lost half of its population in the past half-century, and the city is in desperate need of a re-invention. That was real. According to Marja Winters, aide to Mayor Dave Bing, the essential challenge for everyone involved in the effort to re-invent the city is getting people to think optimistically again. They didn't need more realistic thinking, they needed more optimistic thinking to strike the balance of just the right amount of both.

In a statement attributed to Heaster Wheeler, a former Detroit firefighter who was later the executive director of the Detroit branch of the NAACP, "The best way to predict the future is to create it."

To create a new future, it's helpful to first see the possibilities of that future, which then inspires the action to turn it into a reality. You could also start by taking actions, which may then alter the belief.

Which comes first is the crux of the issue. Sometimes taking initiative gets you moving forward in a positive direction, which shifts your thinking about what is possible. Other times you need to believe before you can get busy doing.

When you have an optimist on your team, or you bring optimistic thinking to your situation, you are more likely to begin the process of building the future that you want.

A realist first sees the work involved to forge that future. He focuses on the lemons. An optimist first sees what can be built in spite of the lemons...or with the lemons.

Sometimes we have to believe in the belief that others have about what's possible for us. That's fine. If you can't find it in yourself to be optimistic, then find someone around you who thinks that more is possible, and believe in them until their belief rubs off on you. It's not bad or wrong to allow the reality of a situation to sink in, but dwelling on it won't get you where you want to go.

People come in two flavors, those who are too hard on themselves and those who are not hard enough on themselves. Take judgment, ego, trying to look good, and trying to prove ourselves out of the equation. Now, perhaps we have a better chance to really see ourselves. Often we view ourselves through a filter of *I'm not good enough* or *I'll find a way no matter what* or some version in between. Neither extreme is good. Before you can deserve more business and earn more money, you must understand the positive and not so positive aspects about what makes you *you*.

Being an optimist is certainly a positive trait, but too much optimism at the expense of a dose of reality may hurt you. Here's what this sounds like in a selling situation:

Prospect: "We love it. We'll find the money."

Salesperson: "Yahoo!"

The salesperson heard these words: "Send the paperwork over later today."

Later that day, after the paperwork is sent over and the champagne is poured...

Prospect: "We're going to have to slow down a bit. I'm not sure where the money will come from."

At this point the salesperson is speechless. He thought he heard *done deal*, but the reality is that he and the prospect never bothered to discern exactly where the money would come from. Their optimism overshadowed the necessity of asking a few more questions to seal the deal.

On the other side of the spectrum is the overly realistic salesperson who can't envision what's on the other side of all the obstacles in the way, so she doesn't even start. The daunting scope of a quota that she doesn't think is realistic throws her into a state of inactivity.

"There's no way that I'll hit that number, so why bother?" Her ego attempts to sabotage her.

Do you have either of these types of people on your team? Maybe you are that person. The highly optimistic folks who score low on reality tests lurk everywhere. They are killing your sales and their own morale, and there is nothing that your motivational trainer can do about it. These people need a dose of reality. *Not an overdose, just the right dose.*

The folks with too intimate a relationship with reality who have lost sight of opportunities need a dose of optimism. *Not an overdose, just the right dose.*

Being upbeat, peppy, and positive has sometimes gotten a bad rap because it is possible to go overboard, and let's face it, that's annoying. Being the one who is always bringing up the worst case scenario is kind of a drag, albeit necessary. Sometimes there is not enough positive, other times there is not enough reality-check. Both can be equally infuriating. So we're going to look at where on that spectrum is just about right. *Be more positive* is a myth because it doesn't take into account where you are right now. If you are already an optimistic, positive person, being more optimistic can hurt you.

Let's consider what happens when an optimist or a realist takes it too far.

7

The Devil's Advocate
And Pollyanna

*You see, lots of times, you get so used to looking for something
to be glad about. And most generally there is something
about everything that you can be glad about,
if you keep hunting long enough to find it.*
~ Pollyanna

No doubt, you've met two kinds of people in your life: the people with gusto and verve aplenty, who always see the silver lining even when the sky is falling and those who walk into a room and the flowers die. Extreme optimists and extreme realists are equally disturbing...and dangerous. Neither is well suited for consistent MVP status. Both have flaws that will keep them from realizing their true potential and discovering possibilities.

The Devil's Advocate is what I call a person who takes their strength of being a realist so far that they are perceived by others as a pessimist. A realist is a person who sees things as they really are, but when taken to the extreme, the perception is that he only sees the negative because there is a tendency to be on the gloomy side. He is the one who not only see the cloud, he's got a story about how the cloud followed him everywhere, drenched him, and that the forecast is for forty days of nothing but rain. The Devil's Advocate is a smashing addition to any party...*that you want to end early.* This guy can tell you all the reasons why something, anything, won't work. He'll tell you why it won't work and what else won't work. With all that brain power poured into what won't work, there's nothing left for thinking up solutions that *will* work.

Having the ability to bring realistic thinking to your opportunities is an admirable skill. It's only an issue when it is perceived by others to be too much of a good thing.

Being the Devil's Advocate is different than *playing* the game devil's advocate to present another side of the story every once in a while. Being a Devil's Advocate means that you are always on the hunt for why things won't work, no matter what the situation is, and you are rarely the one who comes up with new possibilities. It is a sure-fire way to crush possibility thinking.

A pessimist is a person who always anticipates the worst will happen. If you think of yourself as a realist, but take it too far giving others the impression that you are a pessimist… you are what I call Devil's Advocate.

Pollyanna is what I call people who take their strength of an optimistic outlook too far. Pollyanna salespeople, for example, tell their managers that they expect to make their quota, even though they have nothing in their pipeline. You've got to love the spirit of Pollyanna, but the absolute lack of a reality-check gets her into trouble. No need to spend time figuring out how to get there. *I'll get there somehow,* she insists. By casting a spell, maybe?

Pollyanna is usually late because she didn't think that the traffic would slow her down. *Maybe the traffic will disappear by the time I get on the road.* Pollyanna plans trips to the coast during hurricane season because she is convinced that it won't rain on her. Pollyanna sees possibilities, but they don't materialize if it's solely up to her to make them happen. If she does turn a possibility into reality, the result is late or flawed.

An optimist is a person who has a tendency to find the good in everything and to expect the best outcome. If you think of yourself as an optimist, but take it too far and others think of you as a dreamer, you are what I call Pollyanna.

Imagine that it's the seventh grade dance all over again, girls on one side of the gym and boys on the other. In this case, the extreme realists are on the left, and the extreme optimists are on the right.

The music starts playing, and just like the collision of chocolate and peanut butter that gave the world the delicious Reese's Peanut Butter Cup, Pollyanna and the Devil's Advocate meet somewhere in the middle. The Devil's Advocate steps on Pollyanna's toe. Let's listen in...

Devil's Advocate: "I'm so sorry!"

Pollyanna: "No problem, it will be fine in a minute."

Devil's Advocate: "No, it will swell, and you won't be able to walk."

Pollyanna: "I'm fine. I love the added room in my shoe now that one toe is crushed beyond recognition."

Devil's Advocate: "You need to go to a hospital. The toe will have to be amputated."

Then they laughed and fell in love. They grew up, got married, had a baby, and named him Optimist Primarily. Optimist Primarily was about 60 percent optimist and 40 percent realist. What a beautiful baby. The perfect blend of optimism and realism. He could see the light at the end of the tunnel and believed that everything would all work out in the end, but to make sure of it, he processed through the tough questions and did the thinking, the work, and took the action to deal with any possible pitfalls in advance.

If you lean toward being Pollyanna-ish, below are some questions to ponder so that you may balance yourself with some realism:

- What obstacles do I need to see?
- What could go wrong?
- What would I do to deal with adversity?
- Do I anticipate issues in advance?
- What am I not considering that could derail this endeavor?

If you are more of a Devil's Advocate, consider these questions so that you may balance yourself with some optimism:

- What if it did work?
- What is possible here?
- When the work is done, what would be possible that is not possible now?
- If this did not work today, could it work tomorrow?

Over the years I've worked with many of the Pollyannas and the Devil's Advocates of the world. In 2001 I was hired to give the opening keynote for a conference, and the meeting planner was 100 percent Pollyanna. At that time I was new to professional speaking, so I didn't know what I didn't know. She said that she would handle all of the details. All I had to do was show up and test the microphone.

Thinking back on that experience, what tricked me was that she was very detailed in our conversations, so I trusted that she would take care of everything. In reality, far too many things were necessary to produce that kind of an event that she thought she could handle on her own, but did not. Rather than bringing some realistic thinking to the scenario, she relied solely on her optimism, thinking *I can do it!* just like the little engine that could in the storybook.

Sadly, she needed an engine, a coal car, and another caboose to produce a winning event. Well, maybe she didn't really need a coal car, but you get the idea. She kept up her *I can do it* front until it was clear to everyone around her that she couldn't. Fortunately for the attendees of the event, she had an awe-inspiring team of MVPs, all of whom quickly realized that she had taken on too much, and they jumped in and saved the day.

The most effective Pollyannas surround themselves with folks who lean a little more toward being Devil's Advocates.

I learned that when dealing with Pollyannas in my life, it's valuable to shine the light of reality on the situation at hand and make sure that I don't get sucked into their highly attractive rainbows and unicorn plan.

It would have been a perfect ending to the story if the Pollyanna had also seen the need for a shot of reality the next time, but I overheard her say to the members of the team who had rescued her, "I told you that it would all work out just fine!"

Yeah, but it was last-minute and stressed everyone out unnecessarily and was no thanks to her. It doesn't have to be that way. She was still obsessed with hocus pocus thinking about the outcome with no regard for the drama that her planning, or lack thereof, created along the way.

Equally frustrating was a scenario with a client just a few years ago. I was hired to design a new-hire onboarding process for a rapidly-growing sales team in an company with a long sales history. The VP of Sales wanted to document all of the processes that new hires needed to know and be able to execute so that the sales managers in the different regions didn't have to re-invent the wheel. He wanted all new hires to learn a consistent approach.

When I brought together a team of several top-performing sales people to walk me through the steps so that I could blend them together into one best-practices type of process, I met Tom, the most negative high-performer I've ever met.

He answered each of my questions with some version of, *that's the wrong question*. Every suggestion that anyone offered was met with *that's not possible*. I started the session energized, but he drained all the energy out of me.

Why would anyone want to buy anything from this guy? How in the world is he a top-performing salesperson?

What intrigued me about the situation was that it is extremely rare to find a top-performing salesperson who is 100 percent Devil's Advocate. I queried the VP of Sales about the situation.

He scratched his chin. "What? Why was Tom in that session? He's middle-of-the-pack at best."

I had assumed (which is never a good idea), because I had requested to work with a team of top-performers, that everyone in the room fit that description, but the only reason that Tom was there was because his manager had misunderstood the directive.

I bet the VP of Sales $50.00 that I could tell him exactly why Tom was in the middle of the pack in terms of sales results. He took the bet.

I got right to the point. "He doesn't bother calling on new prospects because he's run through the scenario in his own head and has decided the top twenty reasons why they won't buy before he ever picks up the phone to introduce his offer. When someone is interested, he has thirty other reasons why it's not worth his time to follow up because it's never going to happen. When someone else closes a deal he says to himself, 'Yeah, well, customers will never renew, so it was a one-time thing.'"

The VP took $50.00 out of his wallet and handed it to me.

Now that you know about the extreme versions of optimism and realism, let's explore what the mid-range between the two has to offer.

SHIFT STARTERS

- Notice your initial reaction when presented with a new idea. Do you get excited and think that it will work out, or do you want to find the flaws in the idea to make sure that it will work out before you allow yourself to feel enthused?

- Review the questions in this chapter to determine if you lean more toward being a Pollyanna or a Devil's Advocate. Keep in mind how to adjust your usual viewpoint and balance it out.

- Ask several friends or colleagues where they would place you on a spectrum between Devil's Advocate all the way on the left and Pollyanna all the way on the right.

Anchored Optimism 3.3

Realistic optimism does not include or imply expectations that things will improve on their own. Wishful thinking of this sort typically has no reliable supporting evidence. Instead, the opportunity-seeking component of realistic optimism motivates efforts to improve future performances on the basis of what has been learned from past performances. *
~ Sandra L. Schneider, Ph.D.

We're all somewhere on the spectrum between realist and optimist, the Devil's Advocate and Pollyanna. There's a gap there. Somewhere in the middle is just about right.

If the Devil's Advocate is all the way on the left, and we give it a value of one, and Pollyanna is on the far right with a value of five, let's call number two Realist and number four Optimist.

Ideally, you would think that placing yourself in the middle would be the best. From the middle, at point number 3 on our 5-point scale, move a bit toward Optimist, and you'll be firmly planted in the sweet spot, Anchored Optimism 3.3.

Bankers, attorneys, and engineers are in highly-regulated industries, and part of their job is to focus on what could go wrong in order to avoid trouble. There are rules and regulations and processes and structures in these industries. Because of that, sometimes it is difficult to see how something might work out. People in these professions are

* Schneider, S. L. (2001). In search of realistic optimism: Knowledge, meaning, and warm fuzziness. American Psychologist, 56, 250-263.

well-trained to focus on the regulations, the reality, and the rules first. This is perfectly fine, however, these folks should make sure that they don't dip too far to the left into the land of Devil's Advocate.

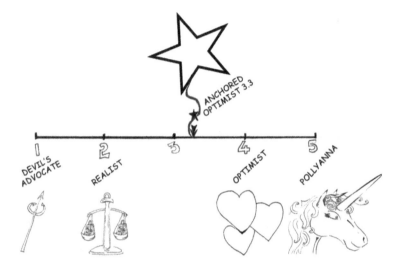

Entrepreneurs, salespeople, entertainers, speakers, and coaches are in the people industry and tend to be on the right side in the land of Pollyanna. They focus on positive outcomes and are sometimes blindsided by adversity.

Options are optimally found in the middle. This is where you have the most power. In the middle, and slightly toward Optimist, is where possibilities are born.

For example, when I'm traveling, I want my pilot to be a Realist, but I also want him to believe that we'll get where we are going. In bad weather I don't want the pilot to be a Realist and say, *We're just destined to have a bumpy ride.* Nor do I want him to be an Optimist and say, *I'm sure that we'll be fine. We'll get there somehow.*

I want him to be in the middle. *There must be a way to avoid the turbulence. What are my options? Can I fly above or below the storm? Can I fly around the storm?* The greatest possibilities for success live in the middle between Realist and Optimist, with a baby step toward Optimist.

On one flight, my overly-realistic pilot actually said, "Grab your air sick bag."

Ugh! Is there an optimist on board? Some people are paid to find the pitfalls in any given situation.

I had a coaching client who was an engineer. His job was to find design faults in order to fix problems before manufacturing began. When he retired, he still found design flaws, with the meal he was eating, the vacation he was on, his son-in-law. Even his granddaughter's Girl Scout leader bore the brunt of his fixation on faults. It's not the job, it's the level of optimism that the person brings to the job.

There is a time for optimism and a time for realism, but the magic is in the middle, which I call Anchored Optimism 3.3. Optimism rooted, or anchored, in realism. The key is to know when to rely on which side of the spectrum.

If you were boarding an airplane in a winter storm, you would want your pilot to be optimistic about reaching the destination, but you would also want him to be a realist and de-ice the plane.

Would you prefer to have a doctor who is an Optimist or a Realist? If your doctor suggested that you undergo major surgery, you would want to know the realistic chances that that would take care of your problem. You would also want her to be optimistic about the outcome.

DR. OPTIMIST

"NO PROBLEM. THE SURGERY WILL GO GREAT AND YOU'LL FEEL GOOD AS NEW!"

DR. REALIST

"YOU COULD DIE. ALL SURGERY IS RISKY. I'LL BE CUTTING YOU OPEN WITH A KNIFE."

DR. ANCHORED OPTIMIST 3.3

"LET'S EXPLORE THE RISKS OF THE SURGERY AND WEIGH THEM AGAINST THE POSSIBILITY OF RELIEVING YOUR CONSTANT PAIN."

So, when is a good time to be an extreme Pollyanna-type optimist who only sees the positive outcome but ignores the realities of the obstacles in the path? I can't think of one. Clearly, I am an advocate of optimistic thinking, but that is distinct from Pollyanna herself. When you are a Pollyanna about things, you only see the good through your rose-colored glasses. These glasses blind you to considering the realistic factors that could derail you. You may put yourself in danger by seeing things from a strictly Pollyanna viewpoint.

When is it good to be a realist? When it is balanced with a healthy dose of optimism. People who err on the side of being overly realistic are just as dangerous as the Pollyannas of the world. Over-achieving realists have walked away from opportunities so often that they have forgotten what it's like to look at the bright side. They are analytical and typically may be detail-oriented, but they only see the black and white of the scenario and rarely look for the shades of gray or the silver lining.

Anchored Optimism 3.3 is what you are striving to achieve for yourself and for your team. Picture a see-saw on the playground, grounded in the middle with two opposite sides, optimism and realism, rocking up and down, attempting to strike a perfect balance.

Imagine that the grown-up sits on the realistic side of the see-saw and the child is on the optimistic side, which is usually how it goes in real life.

Child: "Let's beat the world record for see-sawing!"

Adult: "That would take hours. We wouldn't be able to go to the bathroom or school or work. We'd miss dinner. We don't even know what the current record is."

See how easily the adult goes into realistic mode when someone with optimism crosses his path? It's almost as if he feels that it's his duty to shut someone down, to protect the optimist from getting hurt when they ultimately realize that they can't do what they said they wanted to do. How sad that we've given ourselves the job of CRO, Chief Realist Officer, especially with our children.

My son will figure out on his own the likelihood of his playing in the NFL. There's no need for me to be the voice of reality when he's 13 years old. And who knows at this point what is really possible? Of course, he's going to need to be a bit more realistic about the level of practice that it will take to realize that dream. See, even an optimist like me can grasp the virtues of a reality-check.

Here's another possibility. With Anchored Optimism 3.3, first you get to play along with the optimistic idea. Imagine it working out beyond your wildest dreams. Imagine all the different ways you could get where you want to go. See yourself there. With that new optimistic vision, now you can set your anchor and deal with some reality. When you immediately go to a realistic thought pattern, you shut down possibility thinking. When you allow the realistic considerations to rest on a foundation of optimism, then your reality-check may help you achieve your vision.

On the playground it might sound like this:

Child: "Let's beat the world record for see-sawing!"

Adult with Anchored Optimism 3.3: "Wow! Neat idea. If we broke the world record, we could be famous. Let's see-saw for a while, have some fun, and then go find out what the record is so we can break it."

Optimism that is anchored in reality is the safest, most useful form of optimism. Use your reality-check to help you think through obstacles or roadblocks on your way to your vision. Use realistic data points to determine the weak links in your game plan so that you may plug them up. Use realism, but don't allow it to use you. *Use optimism for its virtues as well, but don't allow it to overtake you.* Overly optimistic people are unprepared. Their extreme optimism hurts them in the long run.

Projects may take longer, the right people are not invited to help with the situation, people may become overwhelmed and overworked when an overly-optimistic leader assesses what needs to be done, by whom, and when. Overly optimistic salespeople think that there is more in the pipeline than there is and don't do the necessary work to keep it full. Overly optimistic people anywhere in the organization may be costly.

Achieving Anchored Optimism 3.3 is not easy for people who have a tendency toward extreme realism or extreme optimism, what we've referred to as the Devil's Advocate or Pollyanna, but it may be done.

For those who lean toward realism, you are almost there. At some point, you would be wise to stop analyzing the shortfalls. Get busy dreaming about what could happen if it did work out, and press pause on worrying about all the reasons something won't work. Allow yourself the gift of imagining a situation turning out even better than you anticipated. Why is that any less possible than the thoughts that you more naturally have about things not working out because of the obstacles in the way?

For those who lean toward optimism, you need to test your facts. You may need to enroll someone to be your reality-check person at first and then observe and learn from their process. Run your ideas past your reality-check person to see if there are details that you haven't thought of that could affect your desired results.

Be careful who you choose as your reality-check person. If that person doesn't have a dose of optimism, you won't be on the same page in creating your possibilities, and you will be extremely frustrated. Someone with a stronger personality may dim the light on what you see as possible.

How do you know where you are on the spectrum between Devil's Advocate and Pollyanna? How do you know when you've achieved Anchored Optimism 3.3?

Pay attention to how you react to a new idea. It could be as simple as choosing a restaurant for dinner.

"Let's go to Outback for dinner." Your spouse is eager to go out at 5:45 on a Friday night in a suburban town.

Do you answer, "I have a final exam tomorrow morning, but let's go anyway. I can cram a little more when we get home."

Or do you say, "Outback doesn't take reservations, and it will take an hour to get a table. No way."

Or do you offer another suggestion. "I'd love to go. While we are waiting for a table, will you quiz me for my final exam tomorrow?"

The first response is Pollyanna optimism. I'll throw caution to the wind, forget the final exam, and just do it. It will all work out, and I have to eat anyway, right?

The second response is too realistic and shuts down the possibility that you could have a nice dinner and get a table quickly.

The third response is Anchored Optimism 3.3. You know that you have to study and that you'll probably wait for a table, but you find a way to make that work in your favor to get the result you want. Sometimes you can have it all. Take that Rolling Stones!

It's not what you have, it's what you do with what you have. Let's pretend that you are operating an efficient team. Somebody is gone for a period of time, and the team is down one person. If the objective is *we still have to make our sales goals in spite of being short one person*, what would be said to the team by people on either end of the spectrum?

The Devil's Advocate, the extreme realist, might object and make an adverse suggestion. "We need to lower the sales goal because of the realities in the marketplace and being short staffed."

Pollyanna might proclaim, "We're down a person, but we've still got this sales goal. It'll work out, somehow we'll get there. I don't know how yet, but I know that we can do it!"

Can you see why the extreme sides of the spectrum are equally dangerous? Imagine if you had an entire team of folks representing only one side.

In this situation, the Anchored Optimist would offer this alternative. "It's going to take some extra effort on our part to pull this off, but I believe that we have the talent to do it. Let's get clarity around our current numbers and how far we have to go to reach our goal.

Then we can talk about the obstacles in our way and come up with some solutions to overcome them and achieve the goal."

Let's pretend that you are an optimist of the Pollyanna variety. You are tasked with adding more people to your team. Because you know that you can handle it even though you may never have hired people before, you don't think you need help because you trust that it will all work out. Naturally, the people you like in your interviews are the same as you. Just like that, two more Pollyannas join the team.

Fast-forward to a team meeting. Everyone is excited about the possibilities and certain that they can do everything on their To Do list in less than one week. Nobody considers the possibility of any hiccups. By the end of the week only a few goals are met, and yet everyone still thinks that the rest will take care of themselves. This team is in desperate need of some critical thinking skills.

Now let's pretend that you are more of a realist. You hire two people who share your strengths of seeing the obstacles, which, from your perspective, is better for business than the *it'll all work out* thinking that you've seen in other organizations.

In your team meeting you share the objectives for the group, and one after the other you hear all the reasons why they won't be met. *This is marvelous* you think, because you're able to address the pitfalls and craft a solution, except that everyone's brains are being used for obstacle-hunting, and there aren't any brain cells left to shape new possibilities and solutions.

By the end of the week nobody has been in action because they don't see a path to the desired outcome, only the obstacles in the way. Nobody wants to start something that they don't think will turn out.

That's why I want your brain to meet in the middle. You need both ways of thinking.

I'm not a proponent of lowering goals to meet the situation. I'm a proponent of looking at all of the possibilities, all of the angles of how we can meet that objective in spite of our current circumstances.

An Anchored Optimist would bring exactly the perspective needed. "Okay we're down a person, we still need to meet our sales goals. But necessity is the mother of invention. What other ways, besides what we would typically do if we were fully staffed, can we come up with to meet those goals? What other possibilities are there? How could we meet those objectives in spite of the current circumstances? What can we do with what we have? We need to take a realistic view of where we are and an optimistic view of where we're going and how we're going to get there."

It's that kind of thinking, if you have just a couple of people, or one other person, with whom you can brainstorm who will meet you in the middle and talk. One other person who comes up with an idea that will lead to a new plan. It might even be a better plan than the one you used previously to reach your business development objectives when you had a full staff.

The point is that you can't think of those new possibilities if you're stuck in either Devil's Advocate or Pollyanna mode. You've got to meet somewhere in the middle to find those possibilities. Ideally, the meeting place is Anchored Optimism 3.3, just slightly right of center toward Optimist.

Think of a situation that is happening now and the team that you have. Are you leaning more one way or the other as a group? What could you do to meet more in the middle to create new possibilities for a particular situation?

As for my son, the future MVP of an NFL Super Bowl championship team, it's my job as a parent to nurture his dreams and help him do the critical thinking to achieve them. Even if he never makes it to the NFL, seeing that as a possibility and doing the work and taking the action to make it a reality is his best shot at one day living his dream. It's also the only way that I can get him to eat his vegetables.

Before we move on to the next myth, I'd like to offer one more example.

Suppose I wanted a piece of chocolate cake. If I used the principles of positive thinking and Pollyanna optimism, I would wish and hope for a piece of chocolate cake to appear. If I added a dose of anchored optimism, I could find the nearest place that sells chocolate cake, call ahead to make sure that this fancy place has a slice with my name on it, and get in my car to go pick it up. Or, if I was feeling really industrious, I could bake the cake myself!

MVPs in business don't rely on strategies of hope or wishful thinking. They make things happen because they see a positive outcome, are unafraid to account for any obstacles, and then they take action. It's not that complicated, but it does take some perspective. The next myth to examine is *Be More Present*, so let's move on to Part IV because being in the present moment isn't always the best place to view a situation. Sometimes you need to shift your vantage point.

SHIFT
STARTERS

In order to shift your outlook and reach a place of Anchored Optimism 3.3 it is important to get a handle on where you are right now.

- Draw a horizontal line across the center of a piece of paper, and to the left of the page write Devil's Advocate. Put a number 1 underneath Devil's Advocate. To the right of the page write Pollyanna, and put a number 5 underneath. Mark the midpoint on the line with the number 3.

- Find the midpoint between Devil's Advocate and number 3. Mark that Realist and number it 2.

- Find the midpoint between Pollyanna and number 3. Mark that Optimist and number it 4.

- Draw a star at the 3.3 spot on the line and label it Anchored Optimist 3.3. That's your new sweet spot. Make it your personal goal to put your name there.

- Add descriptions under each heading that illustrate what you consider to be the characteristics of all five categories: Devil's Advocate, Realist, Anchored Optimism, Optimist, and Pollyanna.

- Jot down the names of the people with whom you work, colleagues, customers, vendors, under the category in which you think they fall.

- Find and mark the point on the line that represents your most typical way of being.

- If you are hiring new people anywhere in your organization, look to see if you have any gaps. You don't need Devil's Advocates or Pollyannas, but make sure that you round out your team with a blend of realists and optimists, ideally Anchored Optimists at the 3.3 point on your piece of paper.

- Make sure that your radar is focused on people with a positive attitude and a realistic plan. It's much easier to teach someone what they need to know about how to do their job than it is to teach them how to be an Anchored Optimist 3.3.

Be More Present

**Unless The Present
Moment Stinks**

PART IV

Myth #4

Be More Present

There are no facts, only interpretations.
~ Friedrich Nietzsche

Photography is something that has always interested me. With my old point-and-shoot camera I used to spend so much time frustrated that I saw the picture that I wanted before the camera snapped the photo. Then I got my first digital single lens reflex camera, and I was hooked. Not only did it take pictures the very moment that I wanted to capture the image, it also allowed me to play with focus.

A friend of mine is an artist, and when he paints a subject he sometimes looks at the objects next to that subject. Rather than looking directly at the subject, he sees what he wants to paint from his periphery. Sometimes he turns his head to see the subject sideways to get another perspective. He wants to see the subject from all angles even if he is just painting in one dimension.

In photography you can adjust the aperture and shutter speed, which makes a difference in how the picture will turn out. I can make the background of the photo sharp or blurred. I can snap a photo of action and get the feel of motion or a split second in time. As the photographer, it's up to me to choose the perspective I want in the photograph.

Perspective is a funny thing. It all depends on where your focus is at the moment. If you and I go to a party and you spend the evening talking with funny, interesting people who laugh at all your jokes, and I spend the evening trapped in a corner talking to the lonely guy who just lost his job and his girlfriend, we are each going to have an entirely different perspective on the same party by the end of the evening.

From your perspective, it was a rockin' good time. From my perspective, it was dull and depressing. We attended the same event, but we each have one of two different perspectives.

What does this have to do with becoming an MVP in business? Everything.

Sometimes we need to take a moment to take a look around and really get perspective on where we are in that moment. MVPs demonstrate evidence that they can get more perspective by watching the present from the vantage point of the future.

You get more of what you focus on, so be in control, and choose your perspective wisely. When you have more perspective, you're seeing more than just what meets the eye. To get more perspective on the present, try examining the situation from the perspective of the future. From a future perspective, the present may appear very different.

Do you put your attention on what you *have* that you want more of or what you lack that you want more of? It's a miniature shift in perspective that makes a huge difference in getting more of what you really do want.

Steve is the sales manager of a technology company. When he and I worked together he was managing seven salespeople. He was frustrated that they were not performing the activities he knew they needed to perform to meet their goals, which is not an unusual sore spot among managers. Steve was always highly self-motivated and assumed that everyone would be motivated the way he was, so he didn't go out of his way to praise people. After all, he had never needed that kind of acknowledgment.

After a discussion about perspective, Steve decided to stop focusing on what the team was not doing enough of and start noticing what they were doing well. He noted that they were following up on warm leads, setting up meetings with prospects and affiliate partners, keeping up-to-date on industry trends, suggesting new sales programs, and setting themselves up for a strong sales year.

As he noticed the good stuff and let his team know that he noticed, he started seeing more activity. With the increase in activity, he saw more results. He knew that more was possible for his team, he just didn't know how to get them to see it for themselves. That's why he had harped on the things that they were not doing. He wanted more for them. He rode them hard.

When he shifted his perspective and found the good in the team, he got more activity out of the team, and they had better results. With their increase in results, they got excited and did even more. It snowballed. Everybody won.

It is a myth that you should always *be more present*. Sure, be more present…unless the present moment stinks. In that case, what helps is a shift in how you see the present moment. Just like a camera, you can choose how you see the present moment which may help you clarify what you want and how you may get there. Often, seeing the present moment from the perspective of the future allows some room for new possibilities to offer themselves and new pathways to take you where you want to go via a somewhat different route.

Sometimes we can't even see another perspective because we have bought into the myth that we should be more present. It's not always up to us to see it clearly, but we need to be open to the possibility that another perspective exists. The only way to access a different perspective is to go beyond the present moment.

One of the best ways of getting a new perspective is to join a mastermind group, be on a peer advisory board, or be a participant in a think tank. I have been actively involved with Vistage International, the largest organization of CEOs in the world, since 1999. It has been incredibly beneficial in my business and personal life. It's where I take my toughest business challenges and where some of the brightest minds in business help me see things in a way that I had not considered.

"None of us is smarter than all of us." My favorite Vistage Chair, Jeff Babcock, likes to remind me of this...often.

When things are going well and people encourage you to *be more present*, it sounds like good advice. But, when you are having a bad day or going through a series of difficult times and others tell you to *be more present*, don't you just want to punch them?

It's a myth that being more present is always the best thing. Sometimes it's okay to check out and let a moment or a feeling or a situation pass. The key is knowing how, when, and why to shift your thinking about this myth. Be more present, unless the present moment stinks.

We've all had ups and downs so let's take a look at what your timeline of life really looks like.

9

Your Timeline Of Life

Don't cry because it's over, smile because it happened.
~ Dr. Suess

There is no shortage of people talking and writing about having balance in life. Frankly, they are selling a concept that you don't want until you are dead. Balance in life looks like this: _____. In the medical profession it is called flat-lining. Trust me, that is not the type of balance you need. Ups and downs are good. They happen in your business, in your relationships, in sales cycles, and in your health.

The key is to see the ups and downs for what they really are, cycles of your life, not permanent conditions of good or bad. Whether you are currently in a good cycle or a not so good cycle, it's hard to see it as a cycle when you are in the midst of it. In order to see for yourself that your life has been made up of a series of cycles, it's best to put it on paper.

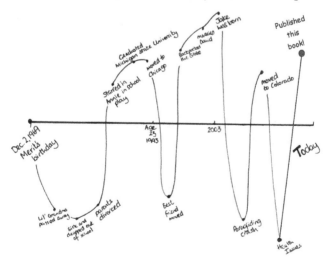

Imagine the timeline of your life, a straight line across the center of a piece of paper. All the way to the left is the day you were born, and all the way to the right is today. If you mapped out the points above and below the line to represent the best and worst times of your life, you would likely see a wavy line with lots of high points and lots of low points. We've all had ups and downs. We've all had exciting things happen in our lives and careers, as well as things that were not so glorious.

For example, the day that I got my first car was a thrilling high point that I plotted on my timeline way above the middle. The day that I crashed that car was way below the center line. Moving across my timeline, I got a different car, I got my first job, and then I was fired from my first job. (*It happens to the best of us. I didn't know about being an MVP in business back then*).

And then I became more Merit, more worthy of praise. I got a new job, a promotion, and things took off from there.

If I focus singularly on that one moment, the day that I crashed the car, I might make decisions about myself or my life. *I'm a terrible driver. I'll never be able to drive. I always ruin a good thing.* I might even make it mean more than that. *Why am I such an idiot, how could I do that?* (This is a terrible question to ask yourself unless you really want your brain to focus on all the reasons why you are such an idiot!) This kind of castigation starts to negatively color the way that you think about everything else on the timeline.

What happened was that I was in a car accident, but if I zeroed in on my whole life through a filter of, *Ugh, this is awful, everything in my life is awful*, then, of course, more awful is coming my way. Even good things that happened would be seen as a fluke, the calm before the storm.

Now, as anybody who's ever gone through any series of ups and downs can tell you, and as I'm sure you've experienced yourself, things do get better, right? They just do. It gets easier. Even the big dips on our timeline of life don't keep us down forever, or at least, they don't have to.

Let's apply this in a business context. You're trucking along, everything's going silky-smooth at work, and then you lose a key employee or a good client. If you've ever experienced that situation, you might recognize it as a low point.

How valuable would it be to your business if you were able to see the situation from the perspective of the future? You might think to yourself, *Huh? Look at that. This is going to be a low point, and for a little while we're all going to have to work our little butts off to make sure that everything runs like it's supposed to. We're going to have to find some new ways to reach our goals. We're going to have to get some perspective on this change.*

From the vantage point of the future you might even recognize the possibility of an even better employee or client filling the current gap, allowing you to key in on the present moment in a whole new light.

If you look over the course of a longer period of time, you might see that you've bounced back after setbacks like this before and that you'll bounce back again. But if you don't have the opportunity to see the situation as a blip in time, if you don't have a way to think with some added perspective, then all you're seeing is that you're in a low point. It's tough to get out of any low point unless you lift your head up and observe the 360 degrees all around you to see what else is possible now.

I delivered a program to a group of branch managers from a nationwide bank shortly after a new regulatory policy called The Telecom Consumer Protection Act (TCPA) prohibited their bankers from calling customers and prospects on their cell phones. This was a problem because many people only use cell phones.

Many of the managers in the room felt defeated by the new regulation and were having some challenges considering new possibilities. By the time we got to the part of the workshop about shifting your thinking about the myth of being more present to having more perspective, I had enough rapport with the group to tell them to stop whining about it. Put it in the past and move forward. Everyone in the industry was dealing with the same issue.

The bankers who found a new pathway to reach their goals would win. To bounce back faster and considerably higher from any adversity is the object of the game, and frankly, as managers, having perspective and bringing more perspective to your team is your responsibility.

If you are leading a team, and they are not naturally wired to get perspective fast, your job as their manager is to help them.

You could say, "Okay, let's move past this present moment, put it in the past and get some perspective here. Change is coming, here's what's happening, let's use a little of our Anchored Optimism 3.3 here so that we may bounce back faster and higher than anybody else in the region. Let's show them what may be done. What are the options that we have to not let this new regulation stop us?"

Perspective is what separates the people who will not bounce back fast from those who will take action and get immediate results. Sometimes being in the present, or worse, stuck in the past is the very thing that will keep you from seeing what's possible in the future.

I suggest that you put it on paper. Anytime you have a setback, draw it out. Draw it out exactly where it would fall in the grand scheme of things. Then, draw what you imagine your next high point will be, and notice that it's on its way to you.

For some people this sounds good in theory, but in reality it's not so easy. Some people have a tough time getting perspective on their own. Some situations are too difficult for people to navigate their way to having more perspective without some extra help. Sometimes it takes the perspective of an outsider to the situation.

Sometimes it makes sense to enjoy the present moment, but other times it's best to let it slip into the past and broaden your present to include your future.

In my personal experiences, when getting perspective isn't coming as easily as I'd like, I get input from a friend, a mentor, a colleague, or a coach. I know exactly which of my friends and colleagues I can go to for help with shifting my perspective.

It's not about doing it on your own, it's about making sure that it's done. When it comes to getting more perspective on a situation, don't try to be a hero. Don't be a lone ranger. Seek the help of others who can see a better future in spite of the present reality.

We all know that Rome wasn't built in a day. It also wasn't built by one person, and if it had been, those people would still be building!

Allow me to take you way back in time to when I was 9 years old and I sold the most Girl Scout cookies in my troop. I couldn't have been more excited, and I looked forward to sewing the new patch on my sash.

At 5:45 p.m., my parents, grandparents, and I filed into the town meeting hall, eager to start the recognition ceremony, in which I was to receive an award. We waited ten minutes, then twenty, then half an hour, for the troop leader to arrive. By 7:00 we gave up.

Two days later we learned that the troop leader had skipped town...with the cookie money. No patches would be given out and no cookies, either! This sordid affair left me with the belief, *Maybe it's best to not put in a lot of effort until you know for sure that everything will work out.*

This experience taught me some crucial, if erroneous lessons. Consciously or unconsciously I believed that if my Girl Scout leader was capable of stealing the cookie money, nobody could be trusted. Ever. That could have led to infinite negative consequences: not trusting business partners, vendors, customers, boyfriends, a spouse (if I could even conceive of trusting a man enough to marry him!). Before I could have a relationship with anybody, I had already decided that it wouldn't work out because they couldn't be trusted, just like my troop leader.

Now imagine that I show up to work in your company. I've done well, and you promote me to manager. To help me in my new role you decide to invest in my management training. I learn how to conduct a review meeting, how to coach people, how to supervise, train, inspire, debrief, strategize, and forecast.

I've been taught the dangers of both micro-managing and not managing enough. I've been given detailed instructions about how to run meetings with people who report to me. But one by one every single person that I manage makes their way into your office to complain about my management style.

Some can't quite put their finger on why I'm not a good manager, others are more direct and they flat-out assert, *It's like she doesn't trust us to do our job.* And they would be right. I have a fundamental belief about people not doing what they say they will do, and no matter what you train me to do, the belief that I developed at age 9 will find that evidence that it needs to keep itself alive every single time. The ego just loves to be right!

If I'm worth keeping as a manager, I have to discover my negative belief and change it. It may be done, and once the belief is re-written or *re-decided*, I may then effectively use what I've learned to be a better manager of people. Until then, you are wasting your time and money training someone with sabotaging beliefs.

Happily, I have put the past in the past where it belongs and I no longer cringe when the cute little Girl Scouts ring my doorbell and sell me too many cookies. By the way, thin mints do not make you thin. False advertising.

At the beginning of this chapter I shared an example of a completed timeline exercise, which shows some of the good and the not so good events in my own life marked by a dot above or below the center line. Now that you have more context for how the past may get the better of you, but it's best not to allow it to run you, take another look at the drawing and use it as a guide to make your own timeline of life.

SHIFT
STARTERS

Now it's your turn to map out your own personal timeline. The purpose is to identify what beliefs you may have generated from past experiences that continue to impact your future.

TIMELINE OF YOUR LIFE

- First, write down the date that you were born all the way on the left of the timeline. Put the current date all the way to the right.

- Next, mark off ten year periods of time and fill in the year under each of these marks. You may certainly use more detailed dates to mark specific events that you easily recall, but starting with decades will help.

- Now, fill in the timeline with events that were positive with a dot above the line and one or two words to describe the event. Then do the same with negative events, except this time put the dot below the line.

- What eventually emerges is a timeline with lots of dots both above and below the center line. What's neat about the timeline is that you begin to see your down cycles as a normal part of living, and you see that ups are sure to follow. Anchored Optimists see these setbacks as a blip in time, not as permanent. Okay, in about twelve minutes you are off to a good start. This exercise allows you to see on paper where you've bounced back before and also that you shall rise again.

- Of course, adversity happens to all of us. You could take this timeline exercise one step further by noticing the belief that you attached to any given experience and the consequences that followed from that belief.

- Pick one dot below the center line.

- In sixty seconds or less write down what happened to you at that time (just like my experience with the Girl Scout cookies). Try to stick to the facts.

- Next, list on a separate piece of paper all of the things that you can think of that someone could believe as a result of that experience, good or bad.

- Look at the list, and put a plus (+) or a minus (–) next to each possible belief, indicating whether it could lead to positive or negative consequences. Put a line through any beliefs that are not really true for you, then look at those remaining.

- What did you decide the event meant in that moment? What did you say to yourself? Is that belief true, or is it a story that you sold yourself so long ago that it still feels true today?

- Do these beliefs from the past creep into your present?

- Note what consequences have developed as a result of the beliefs you adopted.

- If you can live with those consequences, you may keep your beliefs, good or bad. If the consequences are too high a price to pay, then change your belief today.

10

Get Your Cheeks Wet

Life is like riding a bicycle.
To keep your balance, you must keep moving.
~ Albert Einstein

It was a beautiful summer day. My son was 2 years old, and he loved watermelon, so I cut a huge slab for him and one for myself. I was about to tell him how to eat the watermelon from the side and work his way toward the middle so that he didn't get too messy when he took a giant bite from the center. And another and another.

His little cheeks dripped with watermelon juice. I was just about to hand him a napkin and share my motherly words of wisdom.

But he made an unexpected pronouncement. "Mommy, you're doing it wrong!"

Excuse me?

"You gotta get your cheeks wet!" he shouted and buried his face in the center of the watermelon again.

Okay, so this wasn't the picture from that messy-cheek day, but, what the heck, it's my book and I can add a picture of my cute kid if I want to.

Get Your Cheeks Wet is a metaphor that reminds us to be in action, even if it's messy. Do the work. Mistakes are the building blocks of future success. Learn the lessons, then fire up that resilience.

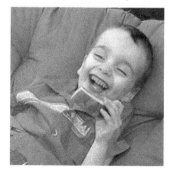

Have you ever been in a situation where someone is trying to help you by telling you what you need to do? Do you ever feel resistant to that? It's so easy to see what others need to do to fix their lives, their sales, their relationships, their bodies, you name it.

But it's not as easy to accept constructive criticism from others ourselves. The reason why it is so difficult is because we often don't hear the constructive part, we only hear the criticism. The more criticism we hear, the more we resist it, even if it is exactly what we need to hear to improve. And it's hard to *get your cheeks wet* and leap into action when you are focused on criticism.

How easy is it to look at someone who is overweight, standing in line to buy ice cream, and think to ourselves, *they shouldn't eat ice cream.* Meanwhile, we are in the same ice cream line, and we haven't worked out for weeks. Hmmm...

How easy is it to tell your co-worker to make more cold calls when your sales are in a slump, and you are not on the phone, either. Hmmm...

My point is that we always have the right advice for others because it's easier to try to fix others than to fix ourselves. Well, it may not be easier to fix them, but it sure is easier to *fixate* on them! If we are fixated on others, this takes the pressure off of us.

If we accept that we are not perfect, then we are admitting that we need fixing. That's not easy for any of us.

So, let's not argue with reality, let's re-frame it. Let's re-decide how we relate to what needs to be perfect. What if your mindset was *there's nothing wrong in my present?*

With that mindset, we are free to get messy and make positive changes because this allows us to move forward rather than trying to fix something that is broken. Rarely is anything wrong, but we see things that do not meet or exceed our expectations.

There was nothing wrong with the way my son ate his watermelon, but I was eager to jump in and fix it, nevertheless.

Expectations are a tricky thing. When we think that something should be a certain way and it doesn't turn out that way, we are more disappointed than if we had never had any idea about how it would go in the first place.

Recently, Stuart, a training and consulting client who owns a company in a service industry, described what I thought was a productive sales call with a new prospect. After the meeting Stuart put together a proposal for twenty-five thousand dollars and thought that he had an excellent chance of closing the deal. When the prospect took a pass on the entire program, Stuart was stunned.

One week later the prospect called Stuart and said that she would like to do a portion of the program. The prospect agreed to a five thousand-dollar deal, and Stuart got started the next day. Normally he was pretty happy with a sale of any size, but this time he was disappointed because his expectations had been set so much higher.

When Stuart told me about the scenario, I encouraged him to re-frame the experience. There's nothing wrong with a five thousand-dollar opportunity that may grow from there. There's nothing wrong with selling a piece of a program, since that not only adds to your bottom line, but it keeps the business from competitors.

There's nothing wrong with not closing the twenty-five thousand-dollar deal right out of the gate. The prospect wants to be sure that you do good work.

I gave Stuart a gentle reminder. "You will feel even better about the project as you grow together."

Intellectually, Stuart knows that when he takes on smaller projects, they often turn into longer-term ones, so instead of being upset that the deal wasn't as big as he originally thought, he re-decided that he was thrilled to begin the project.

There's nothing wrong here, there's nothing that needs fixing. Throughout my life I have said some version of that to myself in all sorts of situations. It keeps me calm, and when I am calm it is so much easier to be resourceful when solutions and alternatives are needed.

When you are upset, when something is wrong, you are usually stressed, and then you don't have access to all of the inventive ways in which you may solve problems.

As my mentor, friend, and therapist, Connie Podesta, told me, "It's as if a part of our brain shuts off the valve that would allow the creative solutions to flow."

The brain is fully focused on what is wrong, leaving no brain function for seeing new possibilities.

When a customer is disappointed in something that he has purchased, do you see it as an opportunity to make a new friend and loyal customer, or do you see it as a problem? Could you shift how you think about the present situation from something is wrong to *there's nothing wrong here?*

My dad took me to a restaurant deli that he goes to often enough that one of the waitresses, Shirley, knows that he likes his fries well done and an extra slice of bread in his favorite sandwich. Waiting for our food, he told me about how he came to order a special sandwich that was not on the menu and how the folks in the kitchen made it for him, anyway.

The first time he ordered his sandwich, it fell apart and wasn't what he wanted. He told Shirley that next time if the chef would put an extra piece of bread in the middle, the sandwich would hold together better. Before he could take the next bite, Shirley whisked the plate away and returned with a new sandwich made exactly how he wanted it.

Shirley's attitude was that there was nothing wrong here, only an opportunity to turn a guy into a loyal customer. She didn't stress out or try to defend the original sandwich. She didn't blame the chef or my dad for ordering something that was not on the menu. She handled it from the perspective of it *not being a problem.*

We may all learn from Shirley, whether we are waiting on tables or selling multi-million-dollar custom manufacturing processes.

Barbara Coloroso, world-renowned speaker and author of parenting books, says that when disciplining our children one of the most important factors is leaving dignity intact for both the parent and the child. If you would not want someone to yell at you, you should not yell at your child. It's the Golden Rule.

She gives an example in her book *Kids Are Worth It* and has you imagine being 70 years old and your adult child telling you, *If you brush your teeth and get dressed without fussing, I'll give you a cookie.* It sounds good when you are the parent of a 7-year-old, but if you reverse the scenario, you probably wouldn't want to be treated in this way when you are 70, so that's your clue that it's not the best tactic to use with your children. (It's also nonsensical to incentivize someone to brush their teeth with the promise of a cookie.)

Her premise is that we need to teach our children to make the right decisions for themselves and have their own internal discipline.

Sales managers may learn a lot from reading good parenting books, but that's a topic for the future. Most managers would prefer not to have to parent at work. For now, we must fortify our own internal discipline, which starts with our mindset and owning up to the attitudes that either support us or sabotage us.

Owning is distinct from knowing. You can *know* something, but unless you *own* that knowledge, nothing will change. When you own it, you take responsibility for it. Some people say that knowledge is power, but I disagree. The knowledge is only powerful if you *own* that knowledge.

For example, do you *know* that you need to lose ten pounds, or do you *own* that you need to lose ten pounds? Do you *know* that you need to save for retirement, or do you *own* that you need to save for retirement? The actions that follow *knowing* something are not of the same caliber as the actions that follow *owning* it.

When you own the knowledge, you are on your way to getting your cheeks wet and being in action in the present. Most of the time people re-decide what needs to change in their lives and from there move on to owning that decision, which leads to action.

In working with business leaders, it is not unusual for them to be overwhelmed with possible scenarios and ways in which to grow their business. Sometimes you make a decision, own that new decision, and get to work only to discover that you made a bad decision and need to re-decide and then start the process all over again.

Perhaps one of the more famous examples on a grand scale was on April 23, 1985, when Coke announced that it was changing the formula of the world's most popular soft drink. The original Coke recipe was not broken, so many would argue, why did the Coca-Cola Company try to fix it?

The soft drink industry was lagging. The company made a decision to introduce New Coke, but the marketplace did not respond favorably.

Over the course of the seventy-nine days after the product went into the marketplace, the people who had brought New Coke to the market accepted responsibility for the error in judgment. They got to work and then re-decided their decision to sell New Coke.

Classic Coke was re-introduced, and the Coca-Cola brand soared to new heights. Incidentally, New Coke, also known as Coke II, is no longer sold in the United States. Think that you can't re-decide something in your world?

These individuals didn't only *know* that they made a mistake, they also owned it. Because they *owned* it, they were able to take the necessary action to make lemonade out of lemons. Or in this case, Classic Coke out of New Coke.

Even when something was wrong, they had to bring an attitude of *there's nothing wrong here*, only an opportunity. It's a subtle but critical shift in mindset. They were willing to get messy and fix the mistake.

Owning up means being willing to say, both publicly and privately, that you want a do-over. In the case of Coca-Cola, if the company's executives had continued to dig their heels in and stick to the original decision to change the formula, this could have been an end to the global brand. Their re-decision reminded consumers how much they love Coca-Cola and re-energized the brand. If Coca-Cola could re-decide on such a grand scale on a world-wide stage, what do you think that you might be able to do?

The one-two punch of re-deciding and owning up is a robust combination. And, it couldn't be more different from changing your mind and seeing how things turns out, which is what many of us do instead.

Every year I used to re-decide my commitment to exercise, but only when I owned that decision did I wake up earlier and sweat for an hour, day in and day out.

Every Monday, George looked at his sales goals for the week and re-decided that he would make five cold calls per day, but it wasn't until he understood the compelling distinction of owning that decision that he actually picked up the phone.

When I share the concept of owning decisions with business leaders and managers, they quickly see the value of asking the people who report to them whether an activity is on their To Do list or if the doing of that activity is something that they really own.

A friend of mine started a business selling title insurance for fine art. It is a unique business. If you have a car and you sell it to your neighbor, you sign over the title to them. The title to the car says that you have the right to sell the car. In the art world, title insurance protects you in case someone sells you a piece of stolen art.

When you own something physical like a car or a piece of art, it has value, and you can prove that you own it with a piece of paper saying that it is so.

When you own the good, the bad, and the ugly about yourself, there is value when you can prove that you own it.

If you are not empathetic and can't put yourself in someone else's shoes, it won't make a difference if you tell someone that you understand where they are coming from. Unless you *own* that *you want to understand their situation*, you will be betrayed by how you listen, and your body language will give you away. With owning your stuff comes a congruency that you don't have until you truly embrace a sense of owning.

This chapter is about getting your cheeks wet and owning the present moment. It is about the shift in mindset between knowing and owning, the shift in mindset between being perfect and getting your cheeks wet.

Of course, sometimes you get into action and things don't go well. Not to worry, you are about to learn how to bounce back from any setback.

SHIFT STARTERS

- Identify an area of your life that you know how to improve, but it's not happening.

- Explore what you would do if you didn't just know what to do but you *owned* that you *could* and *would* do it.

- Look at ways to discover your blind spots. There are many assessments in the marketplace that can shine a light on areas for improvement. One of my personal favorites is the MHS Emotional Quotient Inventory 2.0*. When you own how you show up from an Emotional Intelligence standpoint, you can shortcut your learning curve and begin a path to more influence and effectiveness in any role.

- Own it. Do it.

- Buy a watermelon, cut a gigantic slice for yourself, and get your cheeks wet!

*The team at Merit-based Professional Development is certified in MHS and offers an EQi 2.0 on-line assessment in combination with expert review and follow-up coaching. Please e-mail Support@MeritGest.com to learn more and begin your assessment. In addition, we offer workplace Emotional Intelligence assessments for teams and a Leadership version for management.

11

Bouncing Back To Your Future Faster

The road to success is always under construction.
~ Lily Tomlin

Think of a time when you thought that something was a really big deal in the moment, but later with the benefit of some perspective, you could step back and see it in a new light. We've all had those experiences.

When we moved from Chicago to Denver I was going through some old boxes in an effort to not move a bunch of junk from point A to point B. I found a shoebox full of notes. Remember the notes you passed to your friends in high school? Back in my day, before there were smart phones, we had...what did we call it? Oh, yeah, writing.

Would you like to see one of my notes? Okay, but first you have to go back in your mind to the first day of your senior year of high school. You ruled the school. You knew everything there was to know. Some of you may still think that. You definitely knew more than your parents. The first day of my senior year was in 1986.

I was tired that morning because I had stayed up late watching a new movie, *Back to the Future*. I grabbed my sweatshirt, the one that allowed my shoulder to peek through on one side, and teased my sky-scraping 80s hair. Oh, come on, who else had huge hair and seventy-six black rubber band bracelets? I filled up my gas tank for five dollars (those were the days!) on my way to school, singing *Crazy For You* by Madonna at the top of my lungs.

I was in a rare mood until I got to school. And then my whole world blew up around me. My best friend, Morri, and I passed a note back and forth, but here's what I wrote to her about what happened that day:

Dear Morri,

You will not believe what happened. Today, after three years of going to the same locker in B Hall, the principal announced that we have to move to A Hall! You know what this means, right? I'm not going to see Jon Yanofsky every day! Having our lockers next to each other was our common bond. That's what we were building our relationship on. We had locker language! What am I supposed to do now? What if I'm moved next to a total dork? This is the worst day of my life!

Give me a minute. This seems like it was yesterday.

If you plotted this day on the timeline of your life, where would it be?

At 16 years old, my locker saga was a low point. Today, with a little more perspective, that event wouldn't even register as a blip on my timeline of life events. By plotting the points on a visual display, I can see easily that I've had lots of highs and lows. We've all had wonderful and happy times in our business and personal lives, and we've all experienced exceedingly low points.

Do you know what happens to people who have had a lifetime of ups and downs over time? They become resilient. I think of them like *bounce-back ninjas*. They jump, they roll, and they are stealthy. They get back on their feet and back in action in the blink of an eye, before anyone else does.

The job of a ninja is to cause confusion for the enemy. The enemy on your timeline of life boils down to one word. Failure.

Failure.

It's not the failure itself that stops people in their tracks along the way to becoming a praiseworthy MVP in business, it's that they made it personal. Spell it out loud. F-A-I-L-U-R *(you are)*, and the E is there to remind you that this word is your Enemy.

If a ninja can't get into the building, he doesn't accept failure. The ninja sees it as a setback and assesses the situation to find another way into the building, thereby confusing the enemy.

Examples of people being resilient just prior to massive success dates back many years. Back in 1952, Dr. Norman Vincent Peale published T*he Power of Positive Thinking*, which stayed on the *New York Times* bestseller list for one hundred eighty-six consecutive weeks.

In the book he tells a story about launching a publication called *Guideposts* to promote his theories. The publication had no financial backing, just a borrowed typewriter, a few rickety chairs, and a lot of good intentions. Over time Dr. Peale and his team grew a subscriber list to twenty-five thousand names.

In today's terms, I'm guessing that that would probably be about seventeen million. The future seemed promising. Then a fire destroyed the office that the *Guideposts* staff occupied, and the subscriber list went up in flames. No cloud-based back-up in 1952.

Where would you have put that experience on the timeline of life? Higher or lower than my locker saga?

Dr. Peale was an Anchored Optimist and a bounce-back ninja, so he called a buddy, Lowell Thomas, who happened to host a radio show. Lowell mentioned the flame-broiled subscriber list to his listeners. Instantly the subscriber list went to thirty thousand and soon grew to a quarter of a million subscribers.

The loss of the initial list sparked (pardon the pun) the initiative to build the list in more effective ways. What looked like a setback and a low point was exactly what was needed to create the next higher point.

These types of stories are all around you. Be on the lookout for them. Business is rich with astounding tales of resiliency. MVPs in business effect and collect these stories.

What's your formula for bouncing back after a setback? What questions could you consider yourself? How quickly can you get the perspective you need to turn things around? Who will you go to for help? What could be possible for your career or your life if you recognized every setback as an opportunity to practice your ninja bounce-back skills?

A setback is your opportunity to practice getting back in the game faster and emerging from the setback stronger and more prepared for the success that is on the horizon. Deep down, you know that you can bounce back higher and faster because, as you look at the timeline of your life on paper, you plainly see that you've already experienced setbacks and that another success followed that setback. You've done it before, and you'll do it again, no matter what the setback is.

Perhaps you have heard that our setbacks define us. Humm... sounds like another myth that needs a shift in thinking, but I'll save that for the next book. Setbacks don't define you, (here's the shift in thinking) they outline you. They expand the edges of what is possible and allow you to grow your capabilities. When life is pretty steady, the ups not too high, the downs not too low, you only have to handle what's in the gap. What stretches us and prepares us for higher achievement is the size of the delta between the ups and downs.

We fear setbacks, but that's only because we have not discovered our own bounce-back formula. The highs and lows give us more experiences to draw from to solve challenges in unique ways.

A good friend of mine is a humorist and professional motivational speaker. At the moment, she is going through a nasty, bitter divorce. She's struggling to feel inspiring and funny because she's in the thick of an ugly fight, and she's contemplating her life from the perspective of this dark, low place on her timeline of life.

I reminded her that her timeline extends far beyond this one point and encouraged her to imagine some of the future points on the timeline. Imagining herself from the vantage point of one of those high points, she can look at the low point that she's in now as *not earth-shattering*. Okay, so doing that won't change the nastiness of the moment, but what will change is her relationship to it.

Gazing back on today from a future success means that she may begin to find the sunny spot now. She may focus on the current experiences as valuable lessons that she may learn from to enrich the experiences of her future audiences.

She will be able to go deeper in her future business and personal relationships because this experience has stretched her in ways that she would not have known without it.

That day in high school was a low for me, but fortunately, that one didn't last long because my new locker was right next to Drew Angotti, who was not only the lead in the school musical but also the captain of the football team and way cuter than Jon Yanofsky. By the end of my senior year I was even able to put a few words together to say hello to Drew. And, a mere thirty years later, he friended me on Facebook. *Naturally, I called Morri right away.*

Sixteen years ago I was delivering a sales training program at the Chicagoland Chamber of Commerce. Two young guys who attended the session approached me at the end and wanted to enroll in additional training with me.

At the time they were starting their own business. As they grew their sales skills, they grew their business to the point that they merged their company into a larger company. As part of the deal, they stayed on in leadership roles. Everything seemed fine...until it wasn't. And then they left the business that they had started.

If you asked them about that period of time, they would tell you how disappointing it was to see something that they had built from scratch be operated in a way that was not true to their original vision.

That was not the business plan that they had laid out for themselves or the company that they had envisioned. Fortunately, they also saw the setback as an opportunity to begin again.

Over time, they built another company, and today, as I write this book, they announced an acquisition of their own that makes them a sixty-five-million-dollar company with high profile clients across the country. Ross Freedman and Brad Schneider, owners of Rightpoint, are certainly exemplary examples of bounce-back ninjas.

Now, let's take this idea one step further and also examine the lessons and opportunities offered to us from the positive experiences in our lives. You have certain beliefs about the good things that happen to you as well as the bad. You may go a lot farther a lot faster if you build on your strengths rather than trying to fix your weaknesses.

By looking at your life the way that Brad and Ross do, you'll see that you have bounced back after bad things happen to you. Seeing it on paper helps you recognize setbacks as temporary.

According to Attribution theory, a theory that supposes that one attempts to understand the behavior of others by attributing feelings, beliefs, and intentions to them, those labeled low achievers believe that any success they have is largely due to chance, and they don't acknowledge their own talent or hard work. High achievers believe that their success is due to their ability and effort, and any failure is due to bad luck or something beyond their control. Those who are willing to shift their own thinking about the myths they've been told understand that things happen. But it's the perspective that they bring to what happens that allows any one thing to serve them in a positive way.

It's our perception of the events in our lives that lead us to create possibilities or shut them out. Those who are the MVPs in business put in the extra-credit effort after the primary job is complete, use their Anchored Optimism 3.3 mindset, and practice the art of the bounce-back ninja.

My strategy to deal with setbacks is to visualize or draw a line in the center of a page and plot the point on my timeline of life where this experience feels at that moment. I write a few sentences to help me sort out what is happening and separate the fact from the fiction. I write what is actually happening on one side of the page and what I've made it mean on the other side of the page. I set it aside, sometimes for five minutes, sometimes an hour, sometimes overnight.

Once I've written it down, I try not to think about it. This is especially useful when I have a lot on my plate and it won't serve me to dwell on any issue that takes me off task. Rather than tell myself not to think about it now, writing it on a piece of paper so that I may come back to it later helps my brain get back to where it needs to be. I hold a place in my day to come back to it, but I don't let it take over my brain or my day.

Ideally, I get a little fresh air and move my body in some way, a walk around the block or my office, a quick run up a flight of stairs, or some deep breaths. Next, I identify three people that I may talk to: one person who will listen with empathy; another who may have been there, done that, who will have wisdom to share; and a third who can help me think like a bounce-back ninja and find another way into the building, so to speak.

When I use my bounce-back strategy, I move through setbacks faster. When I am tuned in to the possibilities on the other side of the setback, it is easier to be in motion toward making them happen. When things start happening… let the praise begin.

The question now that you are on the path to being a business MVP is, whose acknowledgment are you after?

SHIFT
STARTERS

- Pick out one business setback that you've mapped on your timeline.

- Identify the high point on your timeline that might not have happened had it not been for that setback.

- What is your setback/bounce-back strategy?

- What usually happens when you are at a low point on your timeline of life?

- Look at the number of times you've bounced back in the past.

- Can you identify the actions that you took or the people who helped you?

- Declare yourself a bounce-back ninja!

In Closing

Whose Acknowledgment Are You After?

Your need for acceptance can make you invisible in this world.
Don't let anything stand in the way of the light that shines
through this form. Risk being seen in all of your glory.
~ Jim Carrey

This book has been all about being an MVP in whatever areas of your life you challenge the truths that sabotage success. MVP salespeople sell more profitable deals with ease and enjoyment. MVP entrepreneurs generate more value for consumers, businesses, employees, vendors, and partners. MVP parents allow space for new and amazing possibilities for their children.

The people whom you acknowledge as MVPs have shifted their thinking about myths that could have sabotaged their success. They have earned your praise because they have taken the initiative to shift their thinking about the business myths that they've been told and gone beyond what was expected of them. MVPs considered what worked and what didn't and had the confidence to re-decide their goals or path when necessary.

People you look up to as MVPs have pondered the tough questions and found a way to stay positive and keep moving toward the goal. People you admire have bounced back from setbacks and have kept things in perspective.

Are there other attributes of MVPs? Of course, but these are the foundation upon which every praiseworthy person or endeavor is noticed.

We've talked about becoming an MVP or identifying what it is that you already do that makes you an MVP, but before you close this book I want to pose some questions, tell one last story, and then challenge you a bit.

First, my questions. Whose praise are you after? Are there several people in a variety of situations? Do you want praise from your boss, your significant other, a parent, your child, a mentor, or a colleague? Do you want or need praise from *yourself*?

Think about it.

Now for the bonus questions. What is the value in stepping up, and what will you lose if you do not step up? What could you lose if you do step up?

Picture a scale with weights on either side. We are always weighing risk versus reward. Is the value of stepping up worth the cost to my relationships or that extra time in the office?

Everybody has it in them to take the next step. What keeps us from executing is the *tall poppy syndrome*.

The *tall poppy syndrome* is a social phenomenon in which MVPs are criticized or resented because of their talents or achievements that elevate them among their peers. Perhaps you know someone who suffers from tall poppy syndrome. You might hear them whisper, *I don't want to rise to top and stand out because I won't get to hang with my friends. I don't want to stay late at the office. I don't want to make mistakes. If I stand out I'll have to do more, or more will be expected of me. What if I stand out and make a mistake?*

You might be excited to step up...and concerned that you won't be able to hang with your friends if you get promoted.

The promotion will help pay for college...but you'll have to travel out of town more, be away from your family.

There are always trade-offs.

Start on either side of the scale. When you do extra credit, you may make mistakes, so you must bounce back fast. When you do extra credit and you're successful, you need to bring your Anchored Optimism 3.3 mindset to new challenges. When you have an Anchored Optimism 3.3 mindset, you look for more extra credit, and the cycle continues. It's easier to do extra credit when you know your formula for bouncing back fast and have a positive outlook.

Business owners see all the things that need to be done, and typically, everyone else zeros in on the specific thing that only they need to do. It's not that they couldn't provide more value, it's that they don't see what needs to be done. Once everyone in the entire company opens their view, it's easier to see how to contribute more.

Any perfectionists out there? It's likely that you have been a perfectionist at some point. Even if it was only when you interviewed for a job and the interviewer inquired about your number one flaw. You said that you're a perfectionist, right? What employer doesn't want something done perfectly?

The problem with perfectionists is that they don't start unless they know that they can finish something flawlessly. If you are managing perfectionists, you need an environment in which it is safe for them to try something, even if it turns out ugly. The more that they are able to say, *It wasn't perfect, but I did it, and here's what I learned*...the more they are willing to keep trying. If they don't have a bounce-back strategy, they may not keep going if what they tried didn't turn out perfectly.

So often, I'm brought into organizations to fix something that is broken: broken sales teams, broken sales processes, broken new-hire onboarding systems, broken spirit. There are no MVPs in sight, and nobody is willing to rise to the occasion.

I hope that your company is on the other side of the spectrum, doing well and clear that more is possible. There is something very special about organizations with a mindset of *More is Possible*, and often all that is needed is to re-connect the people to the possibilities already in front of them.

MVPs are made, not born. My challenge to you is to go out there and make a whole organization full of MVPs and be blown away by the possibilities that they create.

SHIFT
STARTERS

- Who do you want to acknowledge you?
- Write down what you want to be acknowledged for.
- Tell this person why you want their acknowledgment.
- See what happens. Sometimes all you have to do is ask.

Appendix:

For Your Eyes Only:
Current And Future Managers

*We know only too well that what we are doing is
nothing more than a drop in the ocean.
But if the drop were not there,
the ocean would be missing something.*
~ Mother Teresa

The material in this book up to this point was deliberately intended to provide universal messages for anyone in any level of business. Now, I would like to change the focus and speak directly to current and future managers and business leaders because it is going to take something extra on your part to get the most value from the teachings in this book with your team in your organization.

- A high-effort employee may outperform a low-effort employee by 20 percent.

- A strongly-engaged employee is 87 percent less likely to leave a company within the next twelve months.

- An engaged employee is 88 percent more likely to stay even if offered a 10 percent raise for a similar job elsewhere.*

Do I have your attention? Would you like to know how to get more effort and engagement from the beginning when a new employee starts working for you? Would you like to re-board the people you already have on your team?

* McLean & Company

Establishing a culture conducive to cultivating MVPs not only requires people willing to give more of themselves but also an environment favorable to them doing so.

In this special section for managers and leaders, I'm going to share the four things that you may do to set up the environment in which your team may create new possibilities for success.

The four key things that you must do that will improve overall employee performance:

1. Give an employee an early verbal performance review.
2. Explain performance objectives to the employee.
3. Teach the employee about the group or the division in which he or she will work.
4. Clearly articulate his or her job responsibilities.

Likely you've heard all of this before and already have some tools and processes in place to deliver on them. While these key initiatives are also critical in terms of improving the level of discretionary effort that employees are willing to give, research shows that there are some additional activities to consider that specifically impact *the level of that effort* and are often overlooked.

According to the Gallup's State of the American Workplace Report, *more than 70 percent of employees are not engaged at work.* This means that there are roughly four hundred and fifty billion dollars in active disengagement costs in the United States.

How much money is your company wasting, losing, or not recognizing because of low employee engagement and lack of effort?

According to The Recruiting Roundtable and the Corporate Leadership Council, discretionary effort is defined as, *Employee willingness to go above and beyond the call of duty, such as helping others with heavy workloads, volunteering for additional duties, and looking for ways to perform the job more effectively.*

Hmmm. I wouldn't mind a little more discretionary effort at home...

Listed here are four things that all employees want more of, especially your newest hires, consciously or unconsciously, that determine their willingness to give you their best discretionary effort:

1. More opportunities to feel appreciated and valued.
2. More opportunities to fit in with co-workers or the company team.
3. More meaningful work.
4. More tools and resources to be successful in their role in the company.

I bet you thought that more money would make the top four. Nope. Money is nice, and as long as you are paying a reasonable and competitive wage for the work that someone is required to do, they will stay and give you their extra-credit effort as long as the above four criteria are met. It's when there is something lacking in these four areas that people start to wonder what else is out there in terms of employment.

Additionally, while it didn't make the employees' list of the top four things that they want more of from their leaders, we should not underestimate the value of working toward a common goal.

Explaining organizational vision and strategy is important because people will rally behind a cause. If the vision is not clear, the strategy to reach the vision will not be clear. If people can't see where they are going, they won't notice the additional opportunities to get there.

In fact, forget the additional extra-credit effort, they might not be able to execute on their fundamental job responsibilities. And you already know that the extra credit doesn't count if the primary job is not complete. It's as simple as that. Seeing the end goal is one thing, but deciding on the best method to get there is quite another.

Destination Imagination (DI) is a world-wide non-profit organization whose vision is to be the global leader in teaching the artistic process from imagination to innovation. It started in 1982, and since then more than one million people have participated in DI programs.

Every year the DI curriculum designers devise open-ended challenges in the fields of STEM: science, technology, engineering, and math, as well as fine arts and service learning. Teams of young people, from preschool through university, work on innovative ways to solve unique challenges. These kids are given a clearly-defined desired result, but how they get there is up to them.

This program is intended for young people, but adults could benefit from this type of processing and discovery as well.

Let's set up a challenge of your own to get your creative juices flowing. Imagine that you have a box of random materials and were told that your task is to build a structure as tall as possible that will support the weight of a plastic egg.

What if I gave you a box of materials but no explanation about what you are supposed to do with them? This is what companies do when their employees are not privy to the big-picture vision for the organization.

Maybe you would get straight to building. Maybe you would take time to plan and work on a strategy. What would you do? What would your team do? What is the current culture of your organization? Get busy, get messy, mistakes are okay, so start building? Or mistakes are not tolerated so step back, take a breath, and plan?

What if I gave you the outcome that I wanted for the task, build a tall structure to hold the plastic egg, but I didn't give you any materials? Maybe that's good because it opens up a world of possibilities. But maybe it's not good because it leaves too many possibilities, thereby producing chaos, and it would take a long time.

Sometimes, so many things are happening simultaneously within an organization that it's hard for people to know what to focus on to bring their A+ game and accomplish possibly unspecified goals. Many people really want to play at an MVP level, and they want to be recognized for being at that level, but they're not sure how to be successful for you or within the current culture of the organization. They're not sure, there are so many distractions, and there are so many different objectives to accomplish that you, as the leader, need to make the goals and objectives crystal clear in order for everyone to be successful.

Now, what if your company had a culture that didn't consider the myths covered in this book to be true? What if the culture encouraged MVPs in business? What could be possible in that context that is not possible in the absence of that kind of culture? Let's explore the four things that employees want more of from their leaders in a little more depth.

1. More opportunities to feel appreciated and valued.

When my audiences tell me the reasons why they think people leave jobs, most will say that it's because of money or a bad boss. But, when I ask audiences what they think is the most common reason why employees look at what else is out there, many people have answered, *because they don't feel valued or appreciated.* These people are right.

You spend an awful lot of time with the people with whom you work, and if you don't feel valued by them, you leave work feeling empty.

I've always believed that human beings have an *appreciation quotient* to fill every day. If the appreciation quotient is filled by loved ones at home, people go to work happy and can put up with a little more at work because they know that at the end of the day, they are going home to people who value them.

The other benefit to feeling valued at home is that you are probably less likely to find yourself trapped in an unappreciative environment at work. You know better.

But what if you do not feel appreciated at home? How do you meet your appreciation quotient? In that scenario, you would look to fill that void at work. If you feel appreciated at work, you'll love going to work. You'll work nights and weekends willingly because it fills your appreciation quotient in a way that your current personal life does not.

Of course, that's a bit dangerous. I'm not advocating that you spend all of your time working and ignoring the time that may need to be devoted to your personal relationships. Just sayin'...

The fact is that you will enjoy and put more effort into the environment and the people who make you feel most valued and appreciated, wherever that may be.

2. More opportunities to fit in with co-workers or the company team.

Introducing those newly hired to other new employees benefits everyone because you need the camaraderie of a team to reach your aggressive goals. If I like the people I work with, and I know what matters to them, I am more likely to help them out when they need an extra hand. It's always about people. If I like you, I will help you. If I don't like you, I won't help you. *People help people, not departments.*

There is a reason why companies send people to ropes courses for team building. When individuals feel connected to one another, they work harder for and with each other.

Fitting in isn't just important to new hires. It's a basic human need to feel a sense of belonging. Unless you are hiring robots, you'll need to pay attention to the fact that people want to fit in. It's ingrained in us. Human beings are social creatures.

From the time that we first go to school, we're told to make friends, go fit in. Kids who don't fit in have troubles. It's not that they don't fit in, it's that they don't feel like they belong anywhere.

And, in business, that's one of the responsibilities of a manager, to fashion that environment where people feel like they belong.

Sometimes we look at the social activities in which we participate after work as nice-to-haves, little extras. No, they are not extras, they are essential!

We as people are social, we need to connect. I'm not talking about going out for happy hour all the time. Being together in a social setting doesn't have to involve food or drinking, and it doesn't have to involve money. It's also not a gripe session. There are more positive ways to bond with people other than agreeing about what to complain about.

Of equal consideration is how the organization fits in with the community. You may have an opportunity to think, *How can this help us fit in? How can this help my team feel like they belong to their community?* This is a terrific way of thinking.

Find out what the individuals on your team like to do. Do you have a whole team of golfers? Do you have a whole team of scrapbookers? What can you do to foster an environment where people genuinely like each other and want to help each other?

This is critical, whether you are adding a new member to the team or getting the current team to jive together better. Some people bond because they share similar interests. Others bond because of shared experiences. In business, you may facilitate occasions for bonding by presenting opportunities for people to work together.

Perhaps a work team is put together to accomplish a specific task or project. Perhaps a team is put together to organize a social event or a community service project. There are always options to help facilitate relationships, even those that are virtual. Make those events happen.

3. More meaningful work.

Providing meaningful work immediately is necessary because people want to feel useful. They crave a sense of belonging, which they will only get once they are engaged in consequential work. Don't wait to give your people compelling work to do if you don't want them to wait to give you the effort that you desire.

When new people join the company, they are anxious to prove one thing, that you made a good decision in hiring them. They bring an attitude of extra-credit effort because of how it will be seen by others, and there is nothing wrong with this kind of motivation. The team that has been there for a while has settled into their jobs. Unless there is a promotion at stake, they don't have anything to prove, and rarely do they have any incentive to give that extra-credit effort.

It's sad really, because the best reason to give that extra-credit effort is how it makes you feel. You, the person making the extra-credit effort. At some point you've experienced the phenomenon that is extra-credit effort.

You've made that one more call, gotten up early when you were tired, stayed late to beat a deadline. That's the kind of extra-credit effort you see with MVPs who are willing to look at the "truths" they are being told in business and considering for themselves whether they are really true or whether they are myths that will require a shift in thinking to help them reach their goals.

In 1992 I was an account executive for a radio station in Chicago. As the newest member of the sales team and the youngest person on staff, I was eager to prove myself. In addition to selling commercial advertising time, the station was holding an event where advertisers could augment their commercial time with a booth at an expo. I decided that I would focus all of my energy on booth sales.

As the deadline to buy booth sponsorship packages approached, I watched my colleagues on the sales team slow down their efforts. As they put on the brakes, I went into overdrive. In the last three days of the promotion, I sold an additional five booth sponsorships, the last one within minutes of the deadline!

I sprinted back to the office with the signed contract and handed it to my manager just in time to get the client's name printed on the sponsorship flyer. In fact, there wasn't even time for the station to print a banner for the client's booth, so I made one for my late-entry client myself!

Putting in that little bit of extra effort got me noticed among my peers and the executives at the station. I became known as the *new business development pit bull* of our sales force, because once I sank my teeth into a prospect or a contest, I didn't let go until the deal was killed or I'd won.

Within three years I was offered a management role with that station, an opportunity that was not extended to others with more experience, age, and wisdom. Having been given what I considered to be meaningful work spurred me to unforeseen heights. Doing some extra credit early on fast-tracked my entire career.

4. More tools and resources to be successful in their role in the company.

Providing necessary tools and resources is important when you want to increase effort, because you want to help make it easy for people to do what needs to be done. If you wish for a carpenter to build a table but don't give him any power tools, he may get it done, but it will take more time and more effort. All the while he will complain that he could do it faster and easier with the right tools.

Every profession has tools of the trade. It's not always necessary to provide the latest and greatest, especially when technology changes too quickly, but apply your Anchored Optimistic 3.3 thinking and choose the tools that will lead the team to success.

You want people to put in more effort, but you don't want them to put in *unnecessary* effort. You might make a D player out of an A player, and that's not the objective!

∗ ∗ ∗ ∗

Now that you know how to increase an employee's performance and effort, you will be able to get a lot more done...and done well with heart.

What keeps someone from doing the extra credit?

Robert is a graphic designer who works for a design firm that specializes in designs for the hospitality industry. He started as an assistant to a senior designer and VP of the company. He had a commendable work ethic and always wondered what else he could do to help. Time after time he was told that there was nothing extra for him to do, not to worry about it.

But that was not who he was. He was someone who had always gone the extra mile, he always did the extra credit. Even as a young boy, getting A's in school, he did the extra credit.

Eventually he stopped asking what else he could do at work, he just did what he thought needed getting done. Sometimes what he did went unnoticed by anyone else. Sometimes he got a pat on the back, and sometimes he was reprimanded because he made a mistake.

But he kept a positive attitude and saw the setbacks in his life for the blips in time that they were and kept on giving extra effort. He did it because of how it made him feel, and over the course of his life it was a strategy that served him well far more than it ever hurt him.

You would like your team to do the extra credit, even when they have already earned an A, but have you told them that? Have you created an environment in which extra credit is appreciated? Have you given the members of your team an unambiguous, big-picture vision of the goals and objectives for your team, the office, the company overall?

Without sharing a clear vision of the big picture, you are not activating the extra-credit imagination in your people. Not only does this hurt your company, it hurts everyone who doesn't get an opportunity to step into what is possible for them. You rob people of becoming MVPs, and you'll never experience the extraordinary results possible as the leader of a team of MVPs.

* * * *

We've covered a lot of ground together and I'm feeling a bit of pressure to wrap this up with a brilliant summary statement that makes everything click.

At the beginning of the book I devoted one page to a single thought, *Everything is not possible. Choose wisely.*

My intention is that you will choose to be an MVP in all areas of your life and that you will challenge the truths that have sabotaged success for so many. When you do that, more will be possible for you.

Maybe not everything, but a whole lot more.

Acknowledgments

Having ideas is easy. Sharing ideas is easy. Putting ideas together in a book that will have value to readers, a book that is organized and researched and written in your true voice, is not so easy. I would like to acknowledge Paulette Kinnes, who edited this book and kicked my booty when self-doubt kicked mine.

To the woman whose picture was on my vision board for years, and is now a mentor and friend, I could write an entire book about what I learned from the incomparable Connie Podesta. I am forever grateful that she saw something in me and has helped me unleash it.

Though I could write pages about how each of the following individuals have helped me through various stages of my business growth, I'll simply assign the comma between each name to represent my love, appreciation, and admiration for each of them: David Avrin, Jeff Babcock, Hillary Blair, Traci Brown, Sara Canaday, Dr. Rachel Davis, Laurie Guest, Kristina Hall, Christine Hassler, Lou Heckler, Tony Jacobs, Kelly Johnson, Rich Kahn, Tamara Kleinberg, Mark LeBlanc, Elizabeth McCormick, Elaina McMillan, Kevin O'Connor, Meridith Elliott Powell, Lynn Rose, Theresa Rose, Lee Salz, Pandora Slawson, Dawnna St. Louis, Karen Van Cleve, Liz Wendling, Kennen Williams, and Mikki Williams.

Thank you to all of my friends in the National Speakers Association, especially the Colorado chapter, who guide me, teach me, push me, and cheer for me.

Thanks to all of my clients over the past two decades and beyond who have helped me grow as a speaker, coach, trainer, and consultant. If I have achieved expertise it is because you believed in me and allowed me to shine for you.

To my mom, Carole Gordon, and my step-father, Howard, thank you for your unshakable belief in me and for being there when I needed you most.

To my dad, Robert Kahn, who taught me the true meaning of unconditional love and started me on my journey of self-discovery so many years ago.

To my husband David, my Dream Man, my rock when times get tough, I love you more than I thought was possible.

To my son, Jake, everything I do is because I love you. I'm proud of you for no reason at all and for every little thing you do. I love you more than anything.

Finally, to my Little Grandma, Eve Kahn, who has been my guardian angel since I was 7 years old. I think of you every day and hope that I have the same positive impact on people that would have them think of me more than forty years after I have passed on too.

About Merit

Merit Gest has more than twenty years of experience working with companies to grow revenue, increase profitability, and reduce turnover. Merit's work experience and certifications in both Emotional Intelligence and cultural transformation give her a unique perspective regarding hiring, onboarding, selling, and retaining top talent.

Prior to forming Merit-based Professional Development, Merit was the Senior VP of Sales for a nationwide sales training organization and the youngest General Sales Manager for a start-up radio station in the country's third largest market of Chicago.

In her various roles as a business owner, trainer, coach, consultant, and keynote speaker, she has worked with CEOs, business owners, entrepreneurs, and sales management teams, among many others, across a wide variety of industries, including automotive, broadcasting, construction, direct sales, engineering, financial services, healthcare, manufacturing, professional services, real estate, retail, technology, transportation, and even pest control.

Audiences appreciate her humorous delivery and engaging keynotes designed to impact sales, leadership, teamwork, and profitability. She is an active member of The National Speakers Association, has been featured in *Selling Power* magazine as an expert advisor, and is a highly-rated speaker for Vistage International, the world's largest organization of CEOs.

Armed with her Communications degree from Michigan State University and her adventurous spirit, Merit pulls business and life lessons from her experiences backpacking around the world on her own, bungee jumping, sky diving, ice climbing, scuba diving, paragliding, and crashing to the ground from one thousand feet. She may be the only person on the planet who's broken a left foot in Israel and years later a right leg in Croatia and then her wrist on her own street, but somehow she walked away from every incident with inspiring messages to share that allow people an opportunity to find their own personal strength and become an MVP in business and life.

Her husband David is an entrepreneur, real estate developer, expert skier, and Mr. Fix It. They live in Colorado with their son Jake, who is a math whiz, Little Mr. Fix It, and a future Heisman trophy winner.

In her spare time Merit may be found at a day spa (luxuriating the day away!) or at a comedy club...either making the crowd laugh as a stand-up comedian or in the audience enjoying the show!

Book Merit For Your Next Event

Do you need an opening keynote speaker to energize attendees and kick off your conference with inspiration, interaction, and humor? Do you need an emcee who can keep things moving along and inject some belly laughs along the way? Do you need an enthusiastic breakout speaker who doesn't rely on PowerPoint slides to capture the attention of the audience?

Merit Gest delivers relevant content that will grow sales, increase profit margin, inspire leadership, cultivate teamwork, enhance productivity, and achieve world peace. Well, five out of six ain't bad...

She has been described as "the love child between Malcolm Gladwell and Ellen DeGeneres" because she skillfully mixes thought-provoking and actionable content with stand-up comedy and improvisational interaction with the audience.

To book Merit for your next event, conference, corporate meeting, or executive retreat, go to www.MeritGest.com and place a no-obligation hold on your date. Operators are standing by. Well, they're not really standing...

www.MeritGest.com